11/92

· INTRODUCTION ·
TO AFRICAN RELIGION

· Second Revised Edition ·

· JOHN S. MBITI ·

Ph.D. (Cantab.), L.H.D. (h.c. Barrington, U.S.A.)
and D.Theol. (h.c. Lausanne, Switzerland)

Heinemann International Literature and Textbooks
a division of Heinemann Educational Books Ltd
Halley Court, Jordan Hill, Oxford OX2 8EJ

Heinemann Educational Books Inc
361 Hanover Street, Portsmouth, New Hampshire, 03801, USA

Heinemann Educational Books (Nigeria) Ltd
PMB 5205, Ibadan
Heinemann Kenya Ltd
Kijabe Street, PO Box 45314, Nairobi
Heinemann Educational Boleswa
PO Box 10103, Village Post Office, Gaborone, Botswana

LONDON EDINBURGH PARIS MADRID
ATHENS BOLOGNA MELBOURNE
SYDNEY AUCKLAND SINGAPORE
TOKYO HARARE

British Library Cataloguing in Publication Data
A catalogue record for this book
is available from the British Library

ISBN 0435 94002 3

Printed and bound in Great Britain by
Clay Ltd, Bungay, Suffolk

91 92 93 94 10 9 8 7 6 5 4 3 2 1

• Preface

This book is written for three types of readers. Firstly, it is a textbook for use in secondary or high schools and colleges. Secondly, it is for those readers whose formal education reached the level of secondary school or its equivalent. Thirdly, it is for people who do not know anything or much about African Religion. The book is an introduction to that subject and is therefore written in a fairly simple style. Those readers who wish to study at a more advanced level may consult the books given in Appendix B at the end of this book.

Appendix A provides questions on each chapter. These questions may be used in schools or colleges to form the basis for discussions, as exercises or for examinations. It is hoped that teachers in Africa will encourage their students to do some practical studying, where this is possible, of the beliefs and activities connected with African Religion in their own areas. In that way, book learning will be supplemented by field learning.

I wish to express my profound gratitude for secretarial help in preparing the manuscript received from my three secretaries: Mrs Karin Cox, Mrs Frances Mukasa and Mr Joseph Musisi. Since I began to discuss the idea of writing this book, the publishers gave me continued moral support and encouragement, for which I am also very grateful. I am duly thankful to people who allowed me to reproduce their photographs, or to take photographs of religious objects in their possession or care, and in such cases I have made due acknowledgements. Where no acknowledgement is made, the photographs concerned are my own.

• Preface to the Second Edition

Fifteen years have passed since this book, *Introduction to African Religion*, was first published in 1975. During that time the study of African Religion has increased enormously in Africa and beyond, in schools, colleges and universities. Conferences have been held in different countries, in which African Religion, either alone or in connection with other world religions, has been discussed. The number of books and articles published on the subject has also increased. All these are evidence of the value which is attached to African Religion, the appreciation it now receives, and the seriousness with which it is being taken in many places.

This book has become very popular as an introduction to the subject of African Religion. The revised edition is an improvement on the first edition, changing some parts in the light of new knowledge, updating and enlarging the list of books for further reading and the number of photographs. An additional appendix with African proverbs is included, to show the religious and ethical insights contained in oral statements of wisdom. Proverbs are best understood within their linguistic and cultural context, but the space available does not allow us to present that context here. Nevertheless, part of their message will be evident for those who care to reflect further on them or compare them with other proverbs.

I am very grateful to the many people who have reacted positively to this book, and to the publishers for promoting its availability in many countries of the world.

John Mbiti, Burgdorf, Switzerland, 3 August 1990

• Contents

People take their religion with them and in them, wherever they go. In many countries of Africa, vehicles, like the bus below, carry religious slogans, and sometimes the slogans are needed, when drivers speed or drive recklessly!

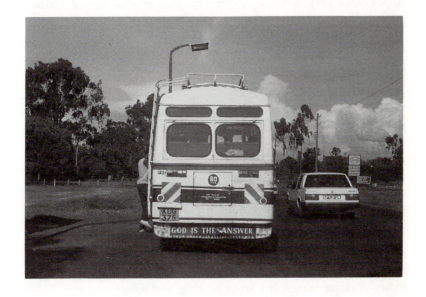

1 · The African Heritage

• The Richness of the African Heritage

Africa has a very rich heritage of what past generations of African peoples thought, did, experienced and passed on to their children. This heritage forms a long line which links African forefathers and mothers with their descendants who now feel proud of it. A study of such a rich heritage makes it possible to see and understand something of the people who lived not only a short while ago, but several hundred or thousand years ago.

Some studies of the origin and development of man have suggested that the earliest men may have lived in East Africa. While this has not yet been fully proved, we may say that if this was the case, then Africa can be considered to be the mother continent or origin of all the peoples of the world. There are traces of early forms of man, found in Ethiopia, Kenya and Tanzania, which date from about two million years ago. In the course of this long history of the presence of man in Africa, many things have happened about which little or nothing is known today. Some things have, however, been preserved through the remains of bones, tools, weapons, and later customs, language, oral traditions, rock paintings, the art of writing, and so on.

In the course of man's long history in Africa, many changes have occurred in ways of living. For a long time, man's source of living depended largely on hunting, fishing and the gathering of wild fruits and honey. At another period he took to farming, agriculture and the keeping of domestic animals. Later on, man began to settle down in villages and towns, of which the earliest known towns are found in the Nile valley of Egypt and Nubia (now the Sudan). Long before people began to live in towns, they started to form into language and ethnic groupings, some of whom migrated to Europe, Asia, the Americas and other parts of the world. In the course of tens of centuries, patterns of living formed along political, social and economic lines, varying from place to place and changing with time.

Thus, the life of man changed gradually from being fairly simple to becoming more and more complex. People adapted their style of living to the environment in which they found themselves, and according to their needs of survival. They developed arts and crafts, acquired new skills and deepened their thinking about the world, their religious and magical ideas spread, they danced and sang, travelled far and wide and moved a long way from the life-style of their first ancestors and previous generations. In short, a great diversity of peoples sprang up everywhere, in Africa as elsewhere. So arose the many peoples of the African continent who have produced their own rich heritage.

• The Spreading of the African Heritage

The African heritage is rich, but it is not uniform. It has similarities, but there are also differences from time to time, from place to place, and from people to people. Some of this heritage originated on African soil; it is, therefore, genuinely African and indigenous. But some developed through contact with peoples of other countries and continents. African forefathers and mothers exported their heritage, or lent it to other peoples of the world; and in return they also learnt something from other peoples.

The African heritage spread westwards across the Atlantic Ocean to South America, the West Indies and North America. This happened chiefly through African slaves who were sold there. They mixed with their masters and indigenous peoples, the (red) Indians, biologically and culturally, by bearing children and in cultural life. After the abolition of slavery in the nineteenth century, most of the people of African descent remained there and became an integral part of those countries. Only a few of them returned to Africa. There is, therefore, a lot of African influence in the cultures of the Western Hemisphere, thanks to the rich heritage brought there by African peoples, who did not give it up or lose it altogether.

Africa has also exported part of its heritage to Europe and Asia, through many centuries of contact with these continents. Geo-graphically, Africa and Europe are very close to each other. Africa and Asia are joined together between the Mediterranean Sea and the Red Sea, and run close to each other along the Red Sea. Trade, political rule and the migration of peoples have been the main links between Africa and these two neighbouring continents. This has gone on for many thousands of years.

Much of the African heritage which was exported to the outside world was cultural and religious. African music, for example, became very popular in the Arab countries in the seventh century A.D. (the time when Islam began). African music has influenced the evolution of popular music and dance in South and North America, and the famous 'Negro Spirituals' of the United States of America are based on African musical heritage and religious feeling. In recent times many of the great artists of Europe and America have studied and copied African art.

We see, therefore, that the African heritage has been of benefit not to the peoples of Africa alone, but also to the world at large. We, too, have profited from our contact with peoples of other continents. Each continent, each people, and each generation has made its contribution to human life in ideas, arts, sciences, learning and response to different situations.

• The Nature of the African Heritage

Let us look more closely at the nature of the African heritage, so that we can get a clearer picture of what it means. We may put it into several categories even if it is not possible to mention in detail each and every aspect of our heritage. These categories will, however, help us to see how vast and rich it is.

The historical heritage

The story of man in Africa is very, very long. It goes back to the very first human beings. But most of that history is unknown to us today, since the art of writing only came much later. We learn something of ancient history by digging up places which were once occupied by early men. This science is known as archaeology. We also learn about early history from the study of animal and plant distribution, as well as by studying languages, human features and habits of life. Once the art of writing was invented – Egypt was one of the places where it was first known – it became possible to make and keep written records. Most of the records were later lost or destroyed, but some have survived to this day. From these we can piece together both the history and the manner of life of past generations.

But most African peoples did not invent an alphabet for the art of reading and writing. Therefore they could not keep written records of their history. Instead, they passed on information from one generation to another, by word of mouth. In some societies there have been special keepers of oral tradition, whose duty was to memorize and recite historical and other relevant information. Many things were forgotten or confused in repeated tellings, but tradition is better than nothing and some valuable information has reached us through this method, though in some cases it is difficult to tell the true from the fictitious.

African history shows that a lot of activities have gone on in our continent for many thousands of years. These include migrations, calamities, wars, invasions, hunting, fishing, food-gathering, domestication of animals, farming, mining, metal work, and settlement in villages and cities. Great empires and kingdoms have arisen and gone, such as those of Ghana, Mali and Songhay in western Africa, the kingdoms of the lower Congo (now Zaire), of the Zulu in southern Africa, of Axum in Ethiopia and Nubia in the Sudan. There have been great civilizations, the first of which evolved in Egypt and continued for many thousands of years. There were other African civilizations in north Africa, in east and central Africa, in the Congo basin, and in west Africa. Some of these existed for a short time and left little trace behind them, while others lasted for more than a thousand years and influenced many people both in Africa and beyond.

We see some traces of these past glories of African empires and civilizations in the works of art and buildings which have survived to this day. For example there are still the great pyramids of Egypt, which were built three to four thousand years ago. There is the

Ancient pyramids of Egypt were constructed primarily for religious purposes as burial places for kings and queens.

Part of the Great Zimbabwe ruins.

Great Zimbabwe in Zimbabwe, itself built five to eight hundred years ago, of which only a few ruins remain today. In the civilizations of west Africa mining industries sprang up, metal goods were manufactured, particularly in gold and bronze, and trade routes were developed across the Sahara desert.

All over Africa are found paintings done on rocks, particularly in caves where formerly some of the people lived or took shelter. Such paintings show the artistic abilities of the people and their chief interests, such as religious ceremonies, hunting, and social life.

By the time European powers entered the interior of Africa in the nineteenth century, the African peoples already had long histories of their own. They had gone through many changes socially and politically. Some of their great empires and civilizations had passed away, making it possible and easy for the inhuman Arab and European slave trade to take place. But there were still some powerful kingdoms such as those in what are now Uganda, Rwanda, Burundi, Ghana, Nigeria and Ethiopia, some of which have survived to this day. African peoples were subjected to foreign rule from Europe, and for a period they were made to forget their heritage or to despise it. This did not continue, however, and Africa is now rediscovering the riches of its heritage. The world is also realizing how many and valuable things Africa has developed in all areas of human life. We will never be able to know the full history of African peoples, but what is coming to light is interesting and important in helping us to understand the experiences and ideas of those who formerly lived in Africa. Their history is the history of present-day Africans, including both their failures and their achievements.

The cultural heritage

Every people has a culture, and culture is changing all the time, whether slowly or rapidly. The word culture covers many things, such as the way people live, behave and act, and their physical as well as their intellectual achievements. Culture shows itself in art and literature, dance, music and drama, in the styles of building houses and of people's clothing, in social organization and political systems, in religion, ethics, morals and philosophy,

Sculpture found in Mexico, Central America, dating from the first millennium B.C. This and other similar ones indicate an African presence and influence in the Americans since ancient times.

7

in the customs and institutions of the people, in their values and laws, and in their economic life. All these cultural expressions influence and shape the life of each individual in his society, and in turn the individual makes a cultural contribution to his community through participating in its life and in some cases through creative work.

Each African people has its own cultural heritage. Some aspects of our cultures are fairly similar over large areas of our continent. There are also many differences, which add to the variety of African culture in general. For example, in many parts of Africa one finds round houses, the keeping of cattle, sheep and goats, and the growing of bananas, millets, or yams as staple foods. The custom of a husband having more than one wife exists in practically every African society. These are only a few examples of cultural similarities in Africa, which make it possible to speak of African culture (in the singular) remembering, however, that there are many varieties of it.

Stories, proverbs, riddles, myths and legends are found in large numbers among all African peoples. They have been handed down orally. Some of them are a record of actual historical events, but most of them are created by people's imaginations. They serve many purposes. Some entertain, others warn; some teach morals, others stimulate the imagination of the listener; some are told as a commentary on people's lives in a given period. Myths are often a way of explaining certain things. For example, some myths explain how death came into the world, others explain the changes in the phases of the moon, and other myths tell how different languages and peoples of Africa came into being. Story-telling is the most common recreation in many homes, especially at night, and all children and young people enjoy it.

In proverbs there is a rich deposit of the wisdom of many generations. Every African society has its proverbs, and wise people know how to use them properly. There are proverbs which teach new things to the hearer and others which warn him against evil conduct; some proverbs are used to encourage people in doing something, while others show what is bound to occur in certain circumstances. Proverbs fit into particular situations of life, and most of them have been formulated from human experiences and reflections throughout the ages. They are, therefore, a major source of African wisdom and a valuable part of African heritage. I have made a collection of some 12,000 proverbs from different parts of Africa. See Appendix C for a few examples of them.

Two kinds of 'speaking' drum (Left Nigeria, Right Zaire).

Africans are very fond of music. Therefore music, dance and singing are found in every African community. We also find many kinds of musical instruments, the commonest being the drum. There are drums of many shapes, sizes and purposes. Some drums are used only in connection with kings and chiefs: these royal drums are often considered sacred and may not be played commonly or by anybody. There are war drums, talking drums, ceremonial drums, and so on. Other musical instruments include xylophones, flutes, whistles, bells, harps, trumpets, lyres, mouth-bows, zithers, fiddles, rattles, and many others. They are made of wood, leather, gourds, bamboo, metal, sticks, tree trunks and even, today, of cans and tins. Music is used in all activities of African life: in cultivating the fields, fishing, herding, performing ceremonies, praising rulers and warriors, hushing babies to sleep, and so on. African music and dance have spread to other continents, as we said earlier. They are one of the chief treasures of the African culture and heritage.

Arts and crafts are common in every African society. Some of the art is decorative, intended to make things look beautiful and attractive. Decorative art is found on stools, drums, shields, spears, pipes, pots, gourds, sticks, baskets, dress or cloth materials, mats, domestic animals and even on people's bodies. There are paintings and carvings on walls and rocks and in caves. But the main purpose or reason of African art is to convey religious feeling and meaning. Therefore it is produced in connection with religious ceremonies and rituals, and some is used in secret societies or in the training of apprentices in various skills and professions.

Crafts include the making of pots, baskets, tools, utensils, spears, shields, bows and arrows, masks and carvings. All these and many others have been produced all over Africa, although some communities are better than others at making different articles. The crafts show people's interests and their ability to produce useful and beautiful things, using the materials available.

There are many other cultural activities, but we cannot deal with them all here. These examples are, however, enough to show what treasures are to be found in our cultures if we look for and study them well.

The religious heritage

Religion is part of the cultural heritage, but we can consider it here separately. It is by far the richest part of the African heritage. Religion is found in all areas of human life. It has dominated the thinking of African peoples to such an extent that it has shaped their cultures, their social life, their political organizations and economic activities. We can say, therefore, that religion is closely bound up with the traditional way of African life, while at the same time, this way of life has shaped religion as well.

Because of its great importance in the life of African peoples, religion should be studied carefully and thoroughly. For that reason, this book concerns itself with the study of African Religion. It will present a general picture of the African Religion which has grown out of the African soil. African Religion was not brought in from the outside. It is also called African Traditional Religion, to distinguish it from any other type of religion, since there are other religions in Africa. Let us now consider the characteristics of African Religion, in order to see what it really means.

2 • What is African Religion?

• The Nature of African Religion

What is African Religion? That is a big question, and this book is written to answer it. In order to profit from reading it, we should first look at the nature of religion in general, and then see how African Religion affects the African way of life. Religion can be seen in five parts. No part by itself constitutes the entire meaning of religion. All these parts must be seen as working together to give us a complete picture. Briefly they are as follows.

Beliefs

These are an essential part of any religion. They show the way people think about the universe and their attitude towards life itself. African religious beliefs are concerned with topics such as God, spirits, human life, magic, the hereafter, and so on.

Practices, ceremonies and festivals

This group of activities is also essential to any religion. Religious practices show how people express their beliefs in practical terms. They include praying, making sacrifices and offerings, performing ceremonies and rituals, observing various customs, and so on. Festivals are normally joyful occasions when people sing, dance, eat and celebrate a particular occasion or event. For example, there are festivals to mark harvest time, the start of the rainy season, the birth of a child, and victory over enemies. We find many religious practices and festivals in African Religion. We will consider many of them in this book.

Religious objects and places

This part of religion covers the things and places which people have set apart as being holy or sacred. They are not commonly used except for a particular religious purpose. There are many such religious objects and places. Some are made by man, but others are taken in their natural form and set apart for religious purposes. Some belong to private individuals and families, while

11

others belong to the whole community in a given region. They include places like shrines, groves, sacred hills or mountains and objects like rivers, amulets, charms, masks, and many others. We shall say more about them later in this book.

Values and morals

This is the part of religion which deals with the ideas that safeguard or uphold the life of the people in their relationship with one another and the world around them. Values and morals cover topics like truth, justice, love, right and wrong, good and evil, beauty, decency, respect for people and property, the keeping of promises and agreements, praise and blame, crime and punishment, the rights and responsibilities of both the individual and his community, character, integrity, and so on. They help people to live with one another, to settle their differences, to maintain peace and harmony, to make use of their belongings, to have a relationship with their total environment. There are differences in the values and morals followed by different peoples of Africa, but many of them are similar. It should also be remembered that they change as the living conditions of people change, but they always remain a necessity in human life. We will say more about African values and morals as we study their traditional religion.

Religious officials or leaders

These are the people who conduct religious matters such as ceremonies, sacrifices, formal prayers and divination. In many cases they are trained men and women. They know more about religious affairs than other people, and are respected by their community. They hold offices as priests, rain-makers, ritual elders, diviners, medicine men, and even as kings and rulers. These officials may or may not be paid for their duties, but in most cases people give them presents and gifts to show their gratitude. Without them, religious activities would neither survive nor function properly, and much of the religious wisdom of the people would be forgotten. They are specialists and experts in religious matters; they are the human keepers of the religious heritage. They are an essential part of African Religion since without them it would grind to a halt and people would not benefit from it in practical terms. We have included a study of them in this book, to see how they are trained and do their work.

These then are the five essential parts which together go to make up a religion. We cannot define a religion by only one or two of its parts. They have to be considered together, because religion is complex. Religion is not made up only of beliefs and practices; it has also objects, values and officials. In this book we shall study all these five aspects of African Religion, in order to give us a full picture of the religious insights which African peoples have acquired and experienced in their own setting and life.

Having considered the parts which help to make up a religion, let us now see how African Religion is related to African peoples, how it developed, and what wrong ideas have been held about it.

• African Religion is Part of the African Heritage

In the first chapter we learnt that the African heritage is very rich. It is historical, cultural and religious. Therefore we can say that religion is part and parcel of the African heritage which goes back many hundreds and thousands of years. African Religion is the product of the thinking and experiences of our forefathers and mothers, that is men, women and children of former generations. They formed religious ideas, they formulated religious beliefs,

King Tutankhamun of Egypt, like many other pharaohs (Kings, rulers) of the Seventeenth, Eighteenth and other Dynasties, was said to have been of African descent.

they observed religious ceremonies and rituals, they told proverbs and myths which carried religious meanings, and they evolved laws and customs which safeguarded the life of the individual and his community.

We cannot understand the African heritage without understanding its religious part. Religion is found in all African peoples. Their different cultures have been influenced very strongly by religion as it is found in each people. The earliest records of African history show that the Africans of ancient Egypt were very religious people. Up to this day, Africans who live according to their traditional ways are also said to be very religious.

Through the ages, therefore, religion has been for Africans the normal way of looking at the world and experiencing life itself. For that reason it is found wherever people are. It is integrated so much into different areas of life that in fact most of the African languages do not have a word for religion as such. They only have words for religious ideas, practices and objects or places. We shall look at these later on in the book, to know exactly what they are.

• African Religion Belongs to the People

Because African Religion developed together with all the other aspects of the heritage, it belongs to each people within which it has evolved. It is not preached from one people to another. Therefore a person must be born in a particular African people in order to be able to follow African Religion in that group. It would be meaningless and useless to try and transplant it to an entirely different society outside of Africa, unless African peoples themselves go there with it. Even within Africa itself, religion takes on different forms according to different tribal settings. For that reason, a person from one setting cannot automatically and immediately adjust himself to or adopt the religious life of other African peoples in a different setting. The peoples of Europe, America or Asia cannot be converted to African Religion as it is so much removed from their geographical and cultural setting.

Since African Religion belongs to the people, when Africans migrate in large numbers from one part of the continent to another, or from Africa to other continents, they take religion with them. They can only know how to live within their religious context. Even if they are converted to another religion like Christianity or Islam, they do not completely abandon their traditional religion immediately: it remains with them for several generations and sometimes centuries. A good example of this is the case of Afro-Americans and Afro-Caribbeans in the Americas and the West Indies. In spite of being suppressed, brainwashed and bombarded with another (and foreign) culture since the days of slavery which lasted up to the nineteenth century, they have retained many elements of their African religiosity to this day.

It is African Religion which gives its followers a sense of security in life. Within that religious way of life, they know who they are, how to act in different situations, and how to solve their problems. This does not mean that African Religion has no weaknesses and no false ideas. But as far as it goes, it has supplied the answers to many of the problems of this life even if these may not have been the right answers in every case. Because it provides for them answers and direction in life, people are not willing to abandon it quickly, otherwise they would feel insecure afterwards unless something else gave them an additional or greater sense of security. When Africans are converted to other religions, they often mix their traditional religion with the one to which they are converted. In this way they think and feel that they are not losing something valuable, but are gaining something from both religious systems.

African Religion functions more on a communal than an individual basis. For example, its beliefs are held by the community; therefore it does not matter much whether or not the individual accepts all these beliefs. The ceremonies are performed mainly in or by a group of the family, by relatives, by the whole population of one area or by those engaged in a common occupation.

African Religion is an essential part of the way of life of each people. Its influence covers all of life, from before the birth of a person to long after he has died. People find it useful and meaningful in their lives, and therefore they let it spread freely. They teach it informally to their children through conversation, proverbs and myths, as well as through practice. Young people also learn about it through participating in religious activities such as ceremonies, festivals, rituals and so on.

Since African Religion belongs to the people, no individual member of the society concerned can stand apart and reject the whole of his people's religion. To do so would mean to cut himself off from the total life of his people. Even if the individual is converted to another religion, this should not mean abandoning his African culture altogether. Where there is no real conflict between African Religion and other religions, the convert retains much of his cultural and religious background as long as he remains within the traditional set-up of life.

• How African Religion was Founded

Some of the world religions like Christianity and Islam have founders who started them. This is not the case with African Religion. It evolved slowly through many centuries, as people responded to the situations of their life and reflected upon their experiences. Many factors must have played a part in its development. These include the geographical environment – mountains, rivers, deserts and forests – the change of the seasons, the powers of nature (such as earthquakes, thunderstorms and volcanoes), calamities, epidemics, diseases, birth and death, and major historical events like wars, locust invasions, famines, migrations and so on. To these must be added man's reflection on the universe, the questions about its origin, the earth and the sky, the problem of evil and suffering, the phenomena of nature, and many other problems.

Religious ideas and practices arose and took shape in the process of man's search for answers to these questions, and as ways of making human life safer and better. They were influenced by human experience and reflection. No doubt many of the ideas and practices were later abandoned when they were found to be inadequate. But, as time went on, these ideas and practices increased in number and spread as the people increased and dispersed. Many religious ideas and practices sprang up simultaneously in different parts of the continent, while others spread through contact among the different societies. For this reason, we find both similarities and differences in African Religion all over the continent. Where religious ideas and practices were borrowed or interchanged, each people adapted them to suit its own requirements. Where people spoke related languages, it was easier for some of the religious ideas and concepts to spread among them than where neighbouring people spoke entirely different languages.

Just as there were no founders of African Religion, there have been no reformers, preachers or missionaries to change it, improve it, or take it overseas to other continents. Changes affecting African Religion have sprung up out of the historical changes in the lives of the people concerned. For example, where one society fought and conquered another and ruled it, no doubt the religious life of the conquerors often left its mark on the life of the conquered people. Where a strong king or chief wished to see new ceremonies or sacrifices made, he no doubt made it obligatory for them to be introduced. In time of danger (such as drought, war or calamity), religious activities revived in order to meet the needs of the time. In such ways, change did come upon African Religion from place to place, and from time to time, through leading personalities of the nation, the intermingling of peoples, and natural necessities. Traditional Religion is open to new ideas, and it must have assimilated ideas in the course of its long history.

• Does African Religion have Sacred Scriptures?

The Bible is the sacred book of Christianity, and the Qur'an is the book of Islam. African Religion has no scriptures or holy books. It is written in the history, the hearts and experiences of the people. Having no sacred scriptures, it has been able to move with the times, and it has produced no religious controversies. People are free to hold different views and beliefs without the danger of being accused of heresy or falsehood. On the other hand, since there are no sacred books, we cannot tell precisely what African Religion may have been five hundred years ago and how far it may differ today from what it was many centuries ago. Therefore we cannot speak of the purity of African Religion, since there is no authority about what it was originally or at any given point in its history.

African Religion is very pragmatic and realistic. It is applied to a situation as the need arises. The followers of African Religion are not bound by any authority which goes back in history. They just follow it as it has been handed down to them by former generations, changing whatever is necessary in order to suit their circumstances of life. In that way some ideas and practices are forgotten for ever, unless they may be retained in some religious objects and myths. Whatever is forgotten is forgotten because the people concerned found it useless for their needs and situations of life. Changes are often brought about by new necessities. On the other hand, since rural life does not often change radically, the main ideas and practices of African Religion must have remained unchanged in general, even if the details may not have remained the same because of the lack of sacred writings.

• Some Wrong Ideas about African Religion

Many books and articles about African Religion have been written by outsiders. In these writings a number of wrong and derogatory things have been said. Even many Africans have been led to use the same wrong terms and hold the same ideas. Let us put right some of these wrong things.

African Religion is wrongly called ancestor worship

This is wrong because Africans do not worship their departed relatives. It is true that departed relatives are believed to continue to live and to show interest in their surviving families. These families may show their belief by building shrines for the departed and placing bits of food or drink there or on the graves, and sometimes mentioning them in their prayers. But these acts of respect for the departed do not amount to worshipping them; they show people's belief that the departed of up to four or five generations should not be forgotten. We showed at the beginning of this chapter that acts of worship (such as sacrifices and prayers) are only a part of African Religion. What is a small part cannot constitute the entire religious system. It is completely wrong to speak of African Religion as 'ancestor worship'.

African Religion is wrongly called superstition

A superstition is a readiness to believe and fear something without proper grounds. We have shown that in African Religion much more than beliefs is involved. Furthermore, these beliefs are based on deep reflections and long experience. They cannot, therefore, be called 'superstitions'. Followers of every religion in the world hold a number of superstitions. But this does not mean that their religion as such is the same as superstition. This also applies in the case of African Religion.

African Religion is wrongly called animism or paganism

Animism means the system of belief and practices based on the idea that objects and natural phenomena are inhabited by spirits or souls. It is true that African peoples in their traditional setting acknowledge the existence of spirits, and that some of the spirits are thought to inhabit objects like trees, ponds, and rocks. There are many stories told about such spirits. This is, however, only a small portion of the many beliefs held in African Religion. Furthermore, it has to be seen in the context of the African view of the world in which God is considered to be supreme, and He has under him spirits and men. To say that there are spirits in the world does not mean that people's religion is only about these spirits. Christianity and Islam also acknowledge the existence of spirits, but neither of them is animism. We have pointed out that belief in the spirits is only part of the system of beliefs found in African Religion, and that as a religion it contains much more than this belief.

Paganism or pagan is sometimes used as a derogatory word to describe Africans who are not followers of either Christianity or Islam. Yet there are many people in Europe and America who do not follow either of these world religions, and are often wholly irreligious, but they are never called pagans. Africans who follow African Religion are deeply religious people and it is wrong and foolish, therefore, to speak of them as pagans, or to regard their religion as paganism.

African Religion is wrongly called magic or fetishism

Outsiders have mistakenly regarded Africans as simply believers in magic. It is true that magic, witchcraft and sorcery feature much in the traditional life of African peoples. But their religion is not constructed around magic. It is much more than that. Africans believe that there is a force or power or energy in the universe which can be tapped by those who know how to do so, and then used for good or evil towards other people. But this is only a part of their belief. It is wrong, therefore, to equate African Religion with magic. Later on in this book we will say more about magic and witchcraft.

Fetishism is a word which came originally from a Portuguese word used by early Portuguese traders and travellers to describe the charms worn by Africans on the west coast of Africa. Since then it has been widely used to cover many other things connected with African religious life. It now connotes something bad and primitive. It is a completely inadequate term to describe African Religion. A charm cannot be a religion, neither can a religion be a charm.

There are other wrong names for African Religion but the ones we have considered are the commonest. We can only say that African Religion is a major religious system in its own right. Like every other religion of the world, it has its own weaknesses as well as strengths. Our concern with it in this book is neither to praise it nor to condemn it, but simply to understand it in the context of African life.

3 • Where African Religion is Found

We have said that there are no sacred writings in African Religion. This raises the question of where one finds it if not in a book. In this chapter we can only give a summary of where to look for and find African Religion if one wishes to observe or study it in practical life.

• African Religion is Found in the Rituals, Ceremonies and Festivals of the People

Africans like to celebrate life. They celebrate events in the life of the individual and the community. These include occasions like the birth of a child, the giving of names, circumcision and other initiation ceremonies, marriage, funerals, harvest festivals, praying for rain, and many others. Some of these rituals and ceremonies are done on a family basis, but others are observed by the whole community. They have a lot of religious meaning, and through their observation religious ideas are perpetuated and passed on to the next generations.

• African Religion is Found in Shrines, Sacred Places and Religious Objects

There are many of these. Some shrines belong to a family, such as those connected with departed members of the family or their graves. Others belong to the community and these are often in groves, rocks, caves, hills, mountains, under certain trees and similar places. People respect such places, and in some societies no bird, animal or human being may be killed if it or he or she is hiding in such places.

At the shrines and sacred places, people make or bring sacrifices and offerings, such as animals, fowls, food, utensils, tools, and coins. They also make prayers there. They regard such places as holy and sacred places where people meet with God.

Some of these religious places are man-made, and may be large enough to look like a big house (which is called a temple). Others are simply natural places which are secluded or situated away from people's homes and fields. Often there are people (priests)

Known as 'the witch tree', there is a legend that a famous medicine woman (Nakayima) used to sit under it and attend to the sick and the barren, curing many of them. It is held to be a sacred tree (Uganda).

21

The Ethiopian and Armharic Alphabet.

(Translated from the German source, zeich *means symbol or sign;* wert *means value or equivalent).*

ÄTHIOPISCH UND AMHARISCH.

Name	Wert	Wert	Wert	Wert	Wert	Wert	Wert
Hoi	ha	hū	hi	hā	hē	hẹ	ho
Lewi	la	lū	li	lā	lē	lẹ	lo
H'aut	h'a	h'ū	h'i	h'ā	h'ē	h'ẹ	h'o
Mai	ma	mū	mi	mā	mē	mẹ	mo
Šaut	ša	šū	ši	šā	šē	šẹ	šo
Res	ra	rū	ri	rā	rē	rẹ	ro
S'at	sa	sū	si	sā	sē	sẹ	so
S'at	ša	šū	ši	šā	šē	šẹ	šo
Qof	qa	qū	qi	qā	qē	qẹ	qo
Bet	ba	bū	bi	bā	bē	bẹ	bo
Tau	ta	tū	ti	tā	tē	tẹ	to
Tšau	tša	tsū	tsi	tšā	tsē	tšẹ	tšo
Kharm	χa	χū	χi	χā	χē	χẹ	χo
Naχas	na	nū	ni	nā	nē	nẹ	no
Naχas	ńa	ńū	ńi	ńā	ńē	ńẹ	ńo
'Alef	'a	'ū	'i	'ā	'ē	'ẹ	'o
Kaf	ka	kū	ki	kā	kē	kẹ	ko
Kh'aph	χ'a	χ'ū	χ'i	χ'ā	χ'ē	χ'ẹ	χ'o
Wau	wa	wū	wi	wā	wē	wẹ	wo
'Ain	'a	'ū	'i	'ā	'ē	'ẹ	'o
Zai	za	zū	zi	zā	zē	zẹ	zo
Žai	ža	žū	ži	žā	žē	žẹ	žo
Yaman	ya	yū	yi	yā	yē	yẹ	yo
Dent	da	dū	di	dā	dē	dẹ	do
Džent	dža	džū	dži	džā	džē	džẹ	džo
Gamel	ga	gū	gi	gā	gē	gẹ	go
Ttait	tta	ttū	tti	ttā	ttē	ttẹ	tto
Tš'ait	tš'a	tš'u	tš'i	tš'a	tš'e	tš'ẹ	tš'o
Ppait	ppa	ppū	ppi	ppā	ppē	ppẹ	ppo
Tsadai	tsa	tsū	tsi	tsā	tsē	tsẹ	tso
Dzappa	dza	dzū	dzi	dzā	dzē	dzẹ	dzo
Ef	fa	fū	fi	fā	fē	fẹ	fo
Eps	pa	pū	pi	pā	pē	pẹ	po

Diphthonge.

Wert	Wert	Wert	Wert	Wert	Wert
kwa	kwi	kwā	kwē	kwẹ	tswa
gwa	gwi	gwā	gwē	gwẹ	fwā
qwa	qwi	qwā	qwē	qwẹ	two
χwa	χwi	χwā	χwē	χwẹ	hālē
lwā	šwā	tšwa	nwa	dwa	hālēlū
mwa	swa	bwa	zwa	ttwa	
mwā	rwā	twa	ywa	tš'wa	

22

The Vei Script (Alphabet) below and over the page, is from Liberia. It was invented by Doalu Dukere in the first half of the nineteenth century.

(Translated from the German source, zeichen means symbol or sign; wert means value or equivalent

VEI-SCHRIFT.

Zeichen	Wert	Zeichen	Wert	Zeichen	Wert	Zeichen	Wert
(glyph)	a	*(glyph)*	dže	*(glyph)*	gbǫ	*(glyph)*	n
(glyph)	ba	*(glyph)*	dži	*(glyph)*	gbu	*(glyph)*	na
(glyph)	bā	*(glyph)*	džo	*(glyph)*	ha	*(glyph)*	nę
(glyph)	bai	*(glyph)*	džǫ	*(glyph)*	hā	*(glyph)*	ni
(glyph)	baṅ	*(glyph)*	džoṅ	*(glyph)*	hā	*(glyph)*	nī
(glyph)	be	*(glyph)*	džu	*(glyph)*	he	*(glyph)*	no
(glyph)	bę	*(glyph)*	e	*(glyph)*	hę	*(glyph)*	nǫ
(glyph)	bē̄	*(glyph)*	ę	*(glyph)*	hi	*(glyph)*	nu
(glyph)	bi	*(glyph)*	fa	*(glyph)*	ho	*(glyph)*	nū
(glyph)	bī	*(glyph)*	fe	*(glyph)*	hu	*(glyph)*	ṅa
(glyph)	bǫ	*(glyph)*	fę	*(glyph)*	i	*(glyph)*	ńe
(glyph)	bọ	*(glyph)*	feṅ	*(glyph)*	ka	*(glyph)*	ńi
(glyph)	bō	*(glyph)*	fi	*(glyph)*	kā	*(glyph)*	ńo
(glyph)	bu	*(glyph)*	fo	*(glyph)*	kai	*(glyph)*	ń
(glyph)		*(glyph)*	fu	*(glyph)*	kē	*(glyph)*	ńa
(glyph)	bili	*(glyph)*	ga	*(glyph)*	kę	*(glyph)*	ńę
(glyph)	da	*(glyph)*	ge	*(glyph)*	keṅ	*(glyph)*	ńo
(glyph)		*(glyph)*	gę	*(glyph)*	ki	*(glyph)*	ńga
(glyph)	daṅ	*(glyph)*	gǫ	*(glyph)*	ko	*(glyph)*	ńge
(glyph)	deṅ	*(glyph)*	gō	*(glyph)*	kǫ	*(glyph)*	ńgo
(glyph)	di	*(glyph)*	gu	*(glyph)*	koṅ	*(glyph)*	nde
(glyph)	do	*(glyph)*	gba	*(glyph)*	kǫ	*(glyph)*	ndo
(glyph)	dō	*(glyph)*	ghā	*(glyph)*	kuṅ	*(glyph)*	o
(glyph)	dǫ	*(glyph)*	gbe	*(glyph)*	m	*(glyph)*	pa
(glyph)	doṅ	*(glyph)*	gbę	*(glyph)*	ma	*(glyph)*	pę
(glyph)	dǫṅ	*(glyph)*	gbi	*(glyph)*	mę	*(glyph)*	pe
(glyph)	du	*(glyph)*	gbo	*(glyph)*	mi	*(glyph)*	pi
(glyph)	duṅ	*(glyph)*	gboṅ	*(glyph)*	mo	*(glyph)*	po
(glyph)	dža	*(glyph)*	gbǫ	*(glyph)*	mu	*(glyph)*	ra la

Zeichen	Wert	Zeichen	Wert	Zeichen	Wert	Zeichen	Wert
[symbol]	re le	[symbol]	sö	[symbol]	liń	[symbol]	we
[symbol]	re le	[symbol]	sö	[symbol]	to	[symbol]	we
[symbol]	ri li	[symbol]	su	[symbol]	lö	[symbol]	wi
[symbol]	ro lo	[symbol]	suń	[symbol]	toń	[symbol]	wo
[symbol]	rö dö	[symbol]	seli	[symbol]	lu	[symbol]	wu
[symbol]	rn lu	[symbol]	sediya	[symbol]	taro	[symbol]	ya
[symbol]	sa	[symbol]	ta	[symbol]	u	[symbol]	ye
[symbol]	se	[symbol]	tä	[symbol]	va	[symbol]	ye
[symbol]	se	[symbol]	te	[symbol]	vi	[symbol]	za
[symbol]	seń	[symbol]	te	[symbol]	vö	[symbol]	zi
[symbol]	si	[symbol]	ti	[symbol]	wa	[symbol]	zo
[symbol]	so	[symbol]	tie	[symbol]	wä	[symbol]	zö

who look after communal places of worship, keep them clean, receive people who come to pray or make offerings and sacrifices, and protect them from desecration or misuse by unauthorized individuals.

Religious articles and objects are many, and we find them in all African societies. Some of them are tied round people's necks, arms, legs and waists. Some are kept in pockets, bags, on house roofs, or gates leading into the homesteads. Other religious objects are swallowed and thought to remain in the stomach; or they are dug into the ground in the houses and fields. There are other religious objects which people hide secretly wherever they may think most convenient. In shrines and sacred places, one finds many religious objects of different kinds, sizes and colours.

Shrines, sacred places and religious objects are outward and material expressions of religious ideas and beliefs. They help people in practising and handing down their religion.

• African Religion is Found in Art and Symbols

We mentioned in the first chapter that arts and crafts are part of the African heritage. Often African art expresses religious ideas. We find it on wood, stools, calabashes, stones, sticks, pots, handicrafts, domestic animals and human bodies. It is also expressed in the form of masks and carvings on wood, ivory and stone.

There are many kinds of symbols. They are found often where

art is found, since they are a part of art. Some are represented by insects, birds, animals, certain trees, figures, shapes and colours of all kinds, masks and carvings. For example, among some people the colour of white is the symbol of death, and when a person has died, relatives smear themselves with white chalk or other substance; and in some areas the chameleon is a symbol of protection and security. In many parts of Africa, the sound of the owl is a symbol of bad omen or death.

Each people has its own symbols, whose meanings are generally known to almost everyone. But there are other symbols which can only be interpreted by a few individuals, as, for example, the symbols used in initiation, divination and secret societies. Religious ideas have created many of the symbols; and in turn the symbols themselves help to communicate and strengthen the religious ideas.

• African Religion is Found in Music and Dance

A lot of African music and songs deal with religious ideas and

Tribal and location marks are common. Some of the marks are on the face, as in this photograph (Nigeria), but others are on the chest, back, stomach, ears or elsewhere on the body. They have religious meaning.

These symbols are some of the more common decorative motifs to be found in traditional African architecture.

practices. The religious rituals, ceremonies and festivals are always accompanied by music, singing and sometimes dancing. Music gives outlet to the emotional expression of the religious life, and it is a powerful means of communication in African traditional life. It helps to unite the singing or dancing group and to express its fellowship and participation in life. Many musical instruments are used by African peoples, as we mentioned in the previous chapter, such as the drum, flute, rattle, whistle and others.

Where African peoples have migrated from one part of the continent to another or to overseas countries, they have often taken their music and dance with them. Through these many religious ideas are also retained and celebrated. This is the case among peoples of African descent now living in North America, South America and the West Indies. Some of them still observe religious festivals with dance and songs whose African words they do not understand, since they were taken there by their slave forefathers from west Africa two or three hundred years ago. That shows how powerful music and dance are, in retaining and spreading religious ideas over wide areas and for a long period.

• African Religion is Found in Proverbs, Riddles and Wise Sayings *(See Appendix C)*

We have said that proverbs provide us with a rich source of African wisdom. Some of these proverbs are religious. They contain religious beliefs, ideas, morals and warnings. They speak about God, the world, man, human relationships, the nature of things and so on. They are set within the cultural and social environment of the people who have produced them and use them. Because proverbs are short, it is easy to remember them. Many people know a lot of proverbs and are skilful in using them at the right moment for the right purpose. Since proverbs are easily passed on from one person to another, we find that many of them go back several generations.

Riddles are used mainly for entertainment and stimulating people's thinking. Some of them also contain religious ideas. Wise sayings are often about the world in general, viewed from religious and moral perspectives.

• African Religion is Found in Names of People and Places

Many African names of people and places have meanings. These meanings are often religious. They are given to mark religious ideas and experiences. For example, in Nigeria the name of Babatunde means 'father returns'. It is given to a male child born immediately after the death of his grandfather. For a girl it is Yetunde, 'mother returns'. The meaning of these names shows the belief that death is not the end of life, and that the departed return to be 'born' in their family (although in fact only some of their features are reborn, and not the entire departed person as such). In Uganda the name Byamuhangi means 'they are of (or for) the Creator'. It is given to a male child by the parents as an indication of their belief that the child belongs to God the Creator. Also in Uganda the name Muwanga means 'the one who puts things in order'. It comes from the legend that one day the sun and moon were fighting and when darkness came over the land the people cried to God for help. Then God sent the divinity Muwanga (son of Wanga) to separate the fighting 'brothers', and put each in its place. This is a religious legend, and there is now a divinity known as Muwanga who symbolizes the idea of order and harmony.

There are many names all over Africa which have religious meanings. Therefore we can say that African Religion is found in people's and places' names. This shows the influence of religion in the life of the people. It also shows that people with such names are in effect religious carriers.

• African Religion is Found in Myths and Legends

Stories, myths, legends and biographies of people are another area where we find African Religion. We said in the first chapter that since there was no writing among African peoples, traditional wisdom and experiences and history were passed down by word of mouth. Therefore, stories, legends and myths became a very important source of information and means of communication. Many religious ideas are found in these oral ways of communication, and every African people has plenty of such stories and myths. For that reason, when people listen to them, or read about them, they are listening to the African religious ideas which may be found in them, and many religious ideas are readily taught and spread through the form of stories, legends and myths.

• African Religion is Found in Beliefs and Customs

Every African people has a set of beliefs and customs. Beliefs are an essential part of religion. Customs are not always religious, but many contain religious ideas. Religion helps to strengthen and perpetuate some of the customs; and in turn the customs do the same to religion.

Beliefs and customs often go together. They cover all areas of life. Beliefs generally deal with religious ideas; customs deal with what people normally approve of and do.

This book will talk about many religious beliefs of African peoples. They cover topics like God, spirits, birth, death, the hereafter, magic, witchcraft, and so on. When we come across African beliefs, we are in fact dealing with African Religion, although religion is much more than its beliefs. The beliefs are handed down from generation to generation, sometimes with modifications. Without them no religion can inspire its followers. Even when people are converted from African Religion to another religion, they retain many of their former beliefs since it is hard to destroy beliefs. Some of the beliefs in African Religion are like beliefs in other religions, but some are completely different.

Beliefs have a lot of influence on people. But some beliefs can be and often are false; yet people stick to them firmly and act accordingly. Therefore, it is good to understand people's beliefs well, because it is these beliefs which influence their behaviour. In addition to religious beliefs there are beliefs in other areas of life like politics, economics, science, and so on. Everyone holds certain beliefs, because we all need one or other kind of belief in our daily life. For example, if a woman did not believe that fire (or heat) would cook her food, she might not be able to provide food for the family every day. If you did not believe that your letter would reach your friend or parents, you would not write it.

Thus, beliefs are very important and essential for every day. African Religion has many beliefs, and by studying them we are able to understand not only the religion but the people who follow it.

• African Religion is Found in all Aspects of Life

We have shown the many areas of African life where we find traditional religion. They lead us to conclude that it is seen in all aspects of life. Therefore, it influences all areas of life. African

Religion has been largely responsible for shaping the character and culture of African peoples throughout the centuries. Even if it has no sacred books, it is written everywhere in the life of the people. To be an African in the traditional setting is to be truly religious. Many scholars agree with what was said in the very first sentence of my book, *African Religions and Philosophy*, that 'Africans are notoriously religious'. In each African society, religion is embedded in the local language, so that to understand the religious life of the people properly, one needs to know their language. In each society there are also individual men and women who have a good knowledge of the religion of their people, and others who are responsible for the performance of religious ceremonies and rituals. These pass on their knowledge to people in general and through training others to carry out the religious life of their community. We shall study something about them later.

We have surveyed the areas in the life of African peoples where their religion is found. Let us now consider the geographical distribution of African Religion over the continent.

• The Geographical Distribution of African Religion

Where do we find African Religion on the continent of Africa? It is to be found almost everywhere. The map shows this. One-third of the continent is predominantly Muslim. This covers northern Africa, the Sahara region and the 'Horn of Africa.' But even within this region, there are many traces of African Religion showing that it has not been completely suppressed by Islam. When Islam first came to our continent in the seventh century A.D. it found African Religion there. The Arabs who colonized parts of the African continent have maintained their own religion, Islam, with its Arabian social and cultural forms. But Africans who were converted to Islam, or forced by occupying Arab conquerors to adopt Islam, did not immediately abandon their traditional religion. In some places it has taken several centuries for African Muslims to leave many, but not all, of their African religious ideas and practices. Often they have only mixed Islam with their own traditional religion.

In the remaining two-thirds of Africa and Madagascar we find strong African Religion everywhere, though less so in Ethiopia, where Christianity has been a powerful religion since about the fourth century. Our study of African Religion in this book will

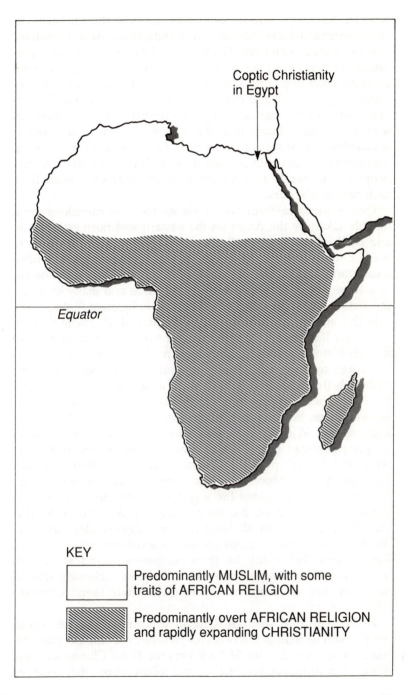

Coptic Christianity
in Egypt

Equator

KEY

Predominantly MUSLIM, with some
traits of AFRICAN RELIGION

Predominantly overt AFRICAN RELIGION
and rapidly expanding CHRISTIANITY

concern this region which covers two-thirds of the continent. In the same area also live the majority of indigenous African peoples. It is a vast area, with over 1500 numerically major African peoples (tribes as they used to be called). It has many geographical contrasts including huge equatorial forests and deserts, great lakes and rivers, sparsely and densely populated areas, about a thousand distinct languages and many more dialects. This region has seen many past civilizations and achievements of African peoples. It includes coastal settlements which for many centuries were in commercial contact with peoples of other lands, as well as interior peoples who hardly had contact with anybody else, apart from their next neighbours.

This is the area from which slaves were so mercilessly and harshly taken by the Arabs on the eastern and northern section, and by the Europeans on the western section, and 'exported' to Asia, Europe and the Americas. It is a region of great mineral wealth and agricultural potential, of floods and locust invasions, of a variety of animals and insects. All these and many more are the factors which prevailed when African Religion took shape.

In this area where African Religion emerged, it remained without major influence from other religions of the world for most of its long history. A few attempts were made three to five hundred years ago to bring Christianity to some of the coastal peoples. Although this was successful in some areas, this success did not last long, nor did it penetrate much into the interior except in one or two places. But from the nineteenth century onwards, Christianity spread in every direction, so that by now every African people has heard the Christian message, and many millions of Africans have accepted the Christian faith. We often find both Christianity and African Religion side by side. In many ways African Religion prepared the way for the conversion of African peoples to Christianity. But their conversion does not mean that they have abandoned all their former religious ideas and traditions. Often their religious life shows a combination of African Religion and Christianity, but there are some who endeavour hard to forsake everything from African Religion, believing that in doing so they are more faithful to their newly found Christian faith.

In the year 1900, African Religion was the largest religion in Africa, with 63 million followers (or 58% of the entire population). Islam came second, with 34.5 millions (or 32%); Christianity was third, with 10 millions (or 9.2%); and followers of other religions including Judaism, Hinduism, Bah'aism, Sikhism, etc., counted about 1 million (1%). Most followers of African Religion started to hear about Christianity in the twentieth century and to convert in larger numbers than those converting to Islam. In 1972 the number of Muslims and of Christians became equal, and thereafter the Christians exceeded the Muslims. In 1984 there were 234 million Christians (that is 45%), 211 million Muslims (or 41%), 63 million (pure) followers of African Religion (or 12%), and 7 million followers of other religions (or 2%). It is estimated that, in the year 2000, Christians will number 394 millions (that is, 48.4%), Muslims 339 millions (41.4%), pure followers of African Religion 72.4% millions (8.9%), and followers of other religions 8.5 millions (1%). It should be remembered that the majority of those who were counted as Christians, and many of the Muslims, still stuck to some of their African religious ideas and practices. Therefore, in effect many millions of Africans are followers of more than one religion, even if they may register or be counted in the census as adherents of only one religion.

Thus, we now have three major religions and many smaller ones in Africa. These are African Religion, Christianity and Islam. Africa is a deeply religious continent, and there is hardly an inch of our continent which does not know this vast religious heritage of not only traditional religion but also world religions. One religion rubs shoulders with another religion in almost every community of Africa today. From the top leaders of our nations to the beggars in our streets, religion plays a role in their lives. Among indigenous Africans, this is often African Religion plus Christianity, and to a lesser extent Islam. Among the African peoples of ancient Egypt (the Copts) and Ethiopia, it is chiefly Christianity. And for the migrants from Europe it is Christianity; among the migrants from Arabia and the Middle East, it is Islam and Judaism; among the migrants from India it is mainly Hinduism, Islam and Sikhism.

That then is the general picture concerning African Religion. Let us take a closer look to see what beliefs it holds, what values it maintains, what views of the universe it cherishes, how it helps people to find a meaning in life and to enjoy that life, what ceremonies it observes and how they link man with God and the unseen world.

4 • African Views of the Universe

• Accumulation of Ideas about the Universe

As they went through life, African peoples observed the world around them and reflected upon it. They looked at the sky above with its stars, moon, sun and meteorites; with its clouds, rain, rainbows and the movement of the winds. Below they saw the earth with its myriad of life-forms, animals, insects, and plants, and its rivers and lakes, rocks and mountains. They saw the limits of man's powers and knowledge, and the shortness of human life. They experienced and witnessed the processes of birth, growth, procreation and death; they felt the agonies of the body and mind, hunger and thirst, the emotions of joy, fear, and love. All their five major senses (of hearing, seeing, feeling, tasting, and smelling) were open gates through which all kinds of experiences came upon them. These experiences stimulated them to reflect upon their life and the universe in which they lived. The result was a gradual building up of African views or ideas about the world and the universe at large.

No thinking person can live without forming some views about life and the world. Some of the ideas developed by individual reflection eventually spread among other people, through discussion, conversation, artistic expression and so on. The other people were stimulated to reflect further, extending old ideas, abandoning some of them, acquiring new ones and translating others into practical realities. And so the process gained momentum, people's ideas about the universe accumulated and definite views and systems of thought began to emerge. There can be no end to the development of people's views about the universe, as this process is a continuing one.

Obviously many ideas about the world have emerged among African peoples. It would be impossible to cover them in detail, but in this chapter we can give a broad summary of them in order to make us familiar with their general content. Their views are expressed in myths, legends, proverbs, rituals, symbols, beliefs and wise sayings. There is no formal or systematized view of the universe, but when these various ideas are put together, a picture emerges. There are many mysteries in the universe and whenever possible people try to find an explanation for them, whether or not the explanation is final.

• A Created Universe

It is generally believed all over Africa that the universe was created. The Creator of the universe is God. There is no agreement, however, on how the creation of the universe took place. But it seems impossible that the universe could simply have come into existence on its own. God is, therefore, the explanation for the origin of the universe, which consists of both visible and invisible realities. People often say that 'God created all things'. In many African languages, the name for God means 'Creator'; even where there is another name. He is often called 'the Creator' as well.

As we will see in the next chapter, the belief in God is found everywhere in Africa. When people explain the universe as having been created by God, they are automatically looking at the universe in a religious way. We can say, therefore, that the African view of the universe is profoundly religious. Africans see it as a religious universe, and treat it as such.

While there are many different accounts of the creation of the universe, it is commonly agreed that man has been put at its centre. We shall see on pages 43–4, that of all created things man is the most important and the most privileged. In some accounts of creation it is told that God made the heavenly part of the universe first, and then, standing on it, he created the earth. In other myths the order is reversed. Some accounts say that the entire universe was created in one act. It is also a widespread view among African peoples that God continues to create. Thus, the creation of the universe did not stop in the distant past: it is an ongoing process which will never end.

• The Nature of the Universe

In many African societies it is believed that the universe is divisible into two. These are the visible and the invisible parts, or the heavens (or sky) and the earth. Some peoples, however, hold that the universe is in the form of a three-tier creation, namely: the heavens, the earth and the underworld, which lies below it. African peoples do not think of these divisions as separate but see them as linked together.

The heavenly part of the universe is the home of the stars, sun, moon, meteorites, sky, the wind and the rain, with all the phenomena connected with them such as thunder and lightning, storms, eclipses of the sun and the moon, 'falling stars', and so on. It is also thought to be the home of God, although people cannot quite locate where he dwells, other than saying that he lives in 'the sky', in 'heaven', or 'beyond the clouds', or they simply say that 'God does not live on the earth like man'. God is often believed to have other beings living with him or close to him. Some of these are in charge of different departments of the universe, others are his messengers and servants or ministers, and some are like his children. But there are other Africans who say that God dwells completely alone and does everything himself, since he is all-powerful.

It is generally held that the heavenly universe is not empty but that it has its own population. It is teeming with its own kinds of life in addition to the visible objects mentioned above. This means that it is more or less the counterpart of the earth, even though what goes on there is invisible to us.

The earth, too, is full of created things. Some African peoples regard it as a living being, and call it 'Mother earth', 'the goddess earth', or 'the divinity of the earth'. Symbolically it is looked on as the mother of the universe, while the heavenly part is the father. In some societies rituals are performed to show respect to the earth. For example, in Zambia, when the rains start, people have to refrain from working on the ground in the fields for a few days. In some parts of Africa when a major calamity like an earthquake or a murder befalls people, sacrifices may be made to the divinity of the earth. On the earth itself many things are held in great esteem for religious reasons, such as mountains, waterfalls, rocks, some forests and trees, birds, animals and insects.

The link between earth and heaven

Man, who lives on the earth, is the centre of the universe. He is also like the priest of the universe, linking the universe with God its Creator. Man awakens the universe, he speaks to it, he listens to it, he tries to create a harmony with the universe. It is man who turns parts of the universe into sacred objects, and who uses other things for sacrifices and offerings. These are constant reminders to people that they regard it as a religious universe.

In many African myths it is told that at one time in the distant past, the heavens (or sky) and the earth were united as one. This union is pictured as being like the place where the earth and sky seem to touch each other at the end of the horizon. Other myths say that the union was formed by a ladder or rope between the two. These accounts go on to say how the separation took place.

According to some, animals bit the leather rope into two, so that one part went up to the sky and the other fell to the ground, thus severing the heavens from the earth. Some myths say that it was through man's fault or error that the two parts of the universe were divided up. These are simply attempts to explain the fact that the universe is divided into two parts, as it appears to be to the ordinary person; and also to explain the fact that God and man are separated.

The universe is seen as eternal

The universe is considered to be unending in terms of both space and time. Nobody can reach the edge of the universe, since it has no known edge or rim. Just as there is no edge of the earth, so there is no edge to the universe. In terms of time, it makes sense for people to believe that there was a beginning for the universe, even though they do not know when it was. But nobody thinks that there will ever be an end to it. They say, 'The world will never end'. African ideas of time concern mainly the present and the past, and have little to say about the future, which in any case is expected to go on without end. Events come and go in the form of minor and major rhythms. The minor rhythms are found in the lives of the living things of this earth (such as men, animals and plants), in their birth, growth, procreation and death. These rhythms are thought to occur in the lives of everybody and everything that has physical life. The major rhythms of time are events like day and night, the months (reckoned on the basis of the phases of the moon), the seasons of rain and of dry weather, and the events of nature which come and go at greater intervals (such as the flowering of certain plants, the migration of certain birds and insects, famines, and the movement of certain heavenly bodies). All these rhythms of time suggest that the universe will never come to a halt, whatever changes there may be.

In many places, circles are used as symbols of the continuity of the universe. They are the symbols of eternity, of unendingness, of continuity. The circles may be used in rituals, in art, in rock paintings, as decorations on stools and domestic utensils and so on. In other places this unendingness is symbolised by drawings of a snake curled round sometimes with its tail in its mouth. The same idea is celebrated in rituals which re-enact birth, death and re-birth, showing that life is stronger than death. This can also be interpreted to mean that continuity on a large scale is more

Some examples of Adinkra patterns and explanations of their significance.

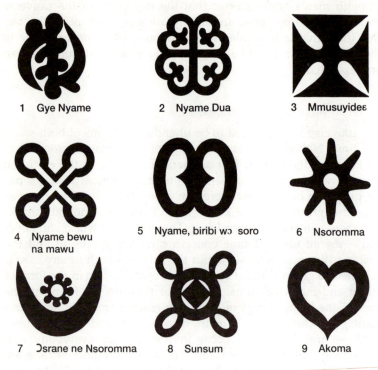

1 Gye Nyame

2 Nyame Dua

3 Mmusuyideε

4 Nyame bewu
   na mawu

5 Nyame, biribi wɔ soro

6 Nsoromma

7 Ɔsrane ne Nsoromma

8 Sunsum

9 Akoma

1 *Gye Nyame (Only God). Symbolises: God almighty, all present and all knowing.*

2 *Nyame Dua (God's tree, a three-forked post planted in home compounds, an altar for God). Symbolises: God's presence everywhere and everytime, hence his protection.*

3 *Mmusuyideε ('thing' for sacrifice). Symbolises: Good omen and uprightness of Spirit, 'wards off negative powers or thoughts'.*

4 *Nyame bewu na mawu (God does not die and so I cannot die). Symbolises: the unending existence of the spirit, as part of God's being or spirit. Hence the continuation of life after death.*

5 *Nyame, biribi wɔ soro (God, there is something in heaven!). Symbolises: God's goodness, reliance on Him to answer prayers. (Ancient Asante kings hung this emblem on palace doors and touched it every morning.)*

6 *Nsoromma (star). Symbolises: We are children of God.*

7 *Ɔsrane ne Nsoromma (the moon and stars). Symbolises: faithfulness, fondness and benevolence; 'dependence of women on men in marriage. Co-operation between the two is essential for success'.*

8 *Sunsum (soul). Symbolises: Purity and spiritual nature of the human being.*

9 *Akoma (heart). Symbolises: fondness, consistency, goodwill and faithfulness.*

10 *Ɔkɔdε mmɔwerε (the talons of the eagle). Symbolises: unity and strength.*

38

| 10 | Ɔkɔdeε mmɔwerε | 11 | Ɛban | 12 | Nkyinkyimiiε | 13 | Kuntinkantan or Kuntunkantan |

| 14 | Akokɔ nan tia ne ba a enkum no | 15 | Hye-wo-ho-nhye | 16 | Bi-nka-bi |

| 17 | Sankɔfa | 18 | Ntesie or Mate masie | 19 | Afuntummireku-Denkyemmireku | 20 | Adinkrahene |

11 Ɛban (fence). Symbolises: safety, security and love.

12 Nkyinkyimiiε (twistings). Symbolises: toughness and selfless devotion to service; an ability to withstand difficulties.

13 Kuntunkantan (Greatness, Pride of State). Symbolises: feelings of Greatness but also warning against inflated ideas about one's self.

14 Akokɔ nan tia ne ba a enkum no (if a hen steps on its chick, the chick does not die). Symbolises: mercy, protectiveness and correction with patience and fondness.

15 Hye-wo-ho-nhye (unburnable). Symbolises: imperishability of self or chief or state.

16 Bi-nka-bi (no one should bite or provoke another). Symbolises: justice, freedom and unity (avoiding strife).

17 Sankɔfa (return and pick it up). Symbolises: a constant reminder that the future may profitably be built on aspects of the past.

18 Ntesie or Mate masie (What I hear, I keep). Symbolises: wisdom, knowledge and prudence.

19 Afuntummireku-Denkyemmireku (the plural headed crocodile with a single stomach). Symbolises: unity in diversity. Democracy, oneness of humanity in spite of cultural diversities.

20 Adinkrahene (king of the adinkra designs). Symbolises: greatness, prudence, firmness and magnanimity.

important than change in small details. People are aware that the laws of nature do not normally change, and so there is no ground for imagining that this entire universe might suddenly come to an end. Thus, the universe is considered to be permanent, eternal and unending.

In the African view, the universe is both visible and invisible, unending and without limits. Since it was created by God it is subsequently dependent on him for its continuity. God is the sustainer, the keeper and upholder of the universe. Man, on the other hand, is at the very centre of the universe, as he has traditionally imagined it to be. Modern science is radically changing that picture. We may summarize these ideas in the form of a drawing:

• Order and Power in the Universe

It is considered that the universe is orderly. As long as this order is not upset there is harmony. Order in the universe is seen as operating at several levels.

Order in the laws of nature

First, there is order in the laws of nature. These function everywhere, and give a sense of security and certainty to the universe. If they were completely unpredictable and changed at random, there would be chaos in the world which would endanger the existence of both life and the universe itself.

Moral order among people

Secondly, there is moral order at work among people. It is believed by African peoples that God gave moral order to people so that they might live happily and in harmony with one another. Through this moral order, customs and institutions have arisen in all societies, to safeguard the life of the individual and the community of which he is part. Moral order helps men to work out and know among themselves what is good and evil, right and wrong, truthful and false, and beautiful and ugly, and what people's rights and duties are. Each society is able to formulate its values because there is moral order in the universe. These values deal with relationships among people, and between people and God and other spiritual beings; and man's relationship with the world of nature.

Religious order in the universe

Thirdly, there is religious order in the universe. We saw earlier on in the chapter that Africans look at the universe in a religious way. Because of their basic belief that the universe is created and sustained by God, they interpret their life's experiences from that starting-point. The laws of nature are regarded as being controlled by God directly or through his servants. The morals and institutions of society are thought to have been given by God, or to be sanctioned ultimately by him. Therefore any breach of such morals is an offence against the departed members of the family, and against God or the spirits, even if it is the people themselves who may suffer from such a breach and who may take action to punish the offender.

There are, therefore, taboos which strengthen the keeping of the moral and religious order. There may be taboos over any aspect of life: words, foods, dress, relations among people, marriage, burial, work, and so on. Breaking a taboo entails punishment in the form of social ostracism, misfortune and even death. If people do not punish the offender, then the invisible world will punish him. This view arises from the belief in the religious order of the universe, in which God and other invisible beings are thought to be actively engaged in the world of men.

Mystical order in the universe

Fourthly, there is a mystical order governing the universe. The belief in this order is shown clearly in the practice of traditional medicine, magic, witchcraft and sorcery. It is held in all African societies that there is power in the universe, and that it comes

The top of the king's authority rod (staff), showing a man and the protective animal (chameleon) (Zaire).

from God. It is a mystical power, in the sense that it is hidden and mysterious. This power is available to spirits and to certain human beings. People who have access to it are sometimes able to see the departed, hear certain voices, see certain sights (such as fire and light), have visions, communicate at a distance without using physical means, receive premonitions of coming events, foretell certain things before they happen, communicate with the invisible world, and perform 'wonders' and 'miracles' which other people may not ordinarily be able to do.

It is the knowledge of this mystical power which is used to help other people (especially in healing, rain-making, finding the cause of misfortunes and troubles, detecting thieves, and so on), or to harm them. When it is used harmfully, it is regarded as evil magic, witchcraft or sorcery; and it may also be used in curses. The ordinary people do not know much about this mystical power. It may take a long time for someone to be trained in the knowledge and use of mystical power; and such knowledge is often safe-guarded and kept secret. In some cases the ability to use this mystical power is simply inherited or passed on without the conscious intention of those concerned. Once a person has dis-covered that he has some of this power, he may then proceed to undertake further training in using it, or he may just neglect it.

• Man at the Centre of the Universe

As the Creator of the universe, God is outside and beyond it. At the same time, since he is also its sustainer and upholder, he is very close to the universe. But in African myths of creation, man puts himself at the centre of the universe. We have already seen the diagram on page 40, showing the central position of man in the universe, according to his pre-scientific image of it.

Because man thinks of himself as being at the centre, he consequently sees the universe from that perspective. It is as if the whole world exists for man's sake. Therefore African peoples look for the usefulness (or otherwise) of the universe to man. This means both what the world can do for man, and how man can use the world for his own good. This attitude towards the universe is deeply engrained in African peoples. For that reason many people have, for example, divided animals into those which man can eat and those which he cannot eat. Others look at plants in terms of what can be eaten by people, what can be used for curative or medical purposes, what can be used for building, fire, and so on. Certain things have physical uses; some have religious uses (for ceremonies, rituals, and symbols); and other things are used for medicinal and magical purposes.

African peoples regard natural objects and phenomena as being inhabited by living beings, or having a mystical life. In religious language we speak of these beings as divinities and spirits. The idea behind this belief is to give man the ability to use or control some of these things and phenomena. For example, if people believe that there is a spirit or divinity of their local lake they will, through sacrifices, offerings or prayers, ask for the help of the divinity when fishing in the lake or crossing it in a canoe. This gives them a feeling of confidence and security, a feeling that they are in harmony with the lake (and with the life-agent personified by the lake or occupying that lake). In some societies it is believed that lightning and thunder are caused by a spirit; therefore people endeavour to be in harmony with that spirit, for fear that it might strike them dead or set their houses on fire.

We may say, therefore, that African people consider man to be at the centre of the universe. Being in that position he tries to use the universe or derive some use from it in physical, mystical and supernatural ways. He sees the universe in terms of himself, and endeavours to live in harmony with it. Even where there is no biological life in an object, African peoples attribute (mystical) life to it, in order to establish a more direct relationship with the world around them. In this way the visible and invisible parts of the universe are at man's disposal through physical, mystical and religious means. Man is not the master in the universe; he is only the centre, the friend, the beneficiary, the user. For that reason he has to live in harmony with the universe, obeying the laws of natural, moral and mystical order. If these are unduly disturbed, it is man who suffers most. African peoples have come to these conclusions through long experience, observation and reflection.

African Religion sees nature as a friend of man and vice-versa. He is an integral part of nature and the priest of nature. The destruction or pollution of nature (including air, water, forests, land, animals, trees, plants and useful insects) brings harm to all life in general and injures human welfare in particular. Therefore, man has to preserve nature and use it wisely, indeed mercifully, for his own and its survival.

5 • Belief in God

• The Origin of Belief in God

All African peoples believe in God. They take this belief for granted. It is at the centre of African Religion and dominates all its other beliefs. But exactly how this belief in God originated, we do not know. We only know that it is a very ancient belief in African religious life. There are three possible explanations of its origin.

People came to believe in God through reflecting on the universe

The belief in God may have arisen from people's reflections concerning the universe. We said in the previous chapter that African peoples believe the universe to have been created. This presupposes that there was a Creator of the universe. That Creator is acknowledged to be God. People realized at a very early date that this vast and complex universe must have had an origin. By using their imaginations they reached the conclusion that there must have been someone who originated it, and it is this someone that they came to consider as God.

In the same way, people reflected on the enormity and continuity of the earth and the heavens. It seemed to them that the universe must have someone who looks after it, keeps it, sustains it. They concluded that the Creator of the universe must also be the one who keeps and sustains it. Without him there could have been no universe, just as without him the universe would have fallen apart.

It became both logical and necessary, therefore, for people to hold a belief in God, as the explanation for the origin and continuity of the universe. It probably took a long time before the belief was formulated so clearly, and there must have been many myths and ideas which tried to explain these mysteries of the world.

People realized their own limitations

The second cause for the origin of the belief in God was probably people's realization of their own limitations and weaknesses. Man saw how limited his powers and knowledge were. This was particularly the case in the face of death, calamity, and the forces of nature (such as thunderstorms, earthquakes, mighty rivers and great forests) which man could not control, or could control only in a very small way. This may easily have led people to speculate that there must be someone greater than themselves and greater than the world, who had full control over it. This idea made it logical and necessary for man to depend on the one who was more powerful than people. Hence, people felt that they needed the help of this one in their experiences of limitation and powerlessness. This one came to be regarded as God.

If this is one of the possible ways that led to the belief in God, again we have to say that it took a long time before the idea could be shaped into its concrete form as we have it now. Some people may first have thought that there were different powers governing the universe, and only later did they reason out that above those powers there must have been one who was or is God. Others may have imagined that just as in human life there are hierarchies of status and power, like babies, children, older brothers and sisters, parents and grandparents; or political hierarchies (with the chief or king at the top), so also there could be a similar hierarchy in the universe at the peak of which was God.

People observed the forces of nature

Thirdly, the belief in God may have been suggested by the powers of the weather, storms, thunder and lightning, and the phenomena of day and night, together with the expanse of the sky with its sun, moon and stars. These heavenly forces, powers and bodies no doubt drew people's attention from the very beginning. People depended on them for light, warmth, rain, and so on. They could not help noticing them, since the sky is so vast and is visible from all over the earth.

People's thoughts were, therefore, drawn towards the sky for more reasons than one. They could not reach the sky. Yet they depended so much on what was in it and what happened there and perhaps beyond it. It is likely that they began to associate the heavens with the one whom they eventually called God. It made sense to them to believe that there was a God, that he lived in the heavens above, and that he was responsible for providing them with the things that are there or come from there. It is no wonder, then, that God is so much associated with the sky and the heavens.

It is very likely that people came to believe in God's existence through such a link between heaven and earth. Man was at the centre of the universe, standing on the earth but looking up to the heavens as well. In looking towards the sky, he formed his belief in God, and that belief began to make sense and fit into man's continued attempts to understand and explain the visible and the invisible universe, the earthly and heavenly worlds of which man is the centre. Ever since, African Religion has evolved around that belief. Let us now see what it says about the work and nature of God.

• The Names of God

Every African people has a word for God and often other names which describe him. Many of the names have meanings, showing us what people think about him. The personal names for God are very ancient, and in many cases their meanings are no longer known or easily traceable through language analysis. Here are some examples of names for God.

Country	Some African names for God
Angola	Kalunga, Nzambi, Suku
Burkina Faso	Na'angmin
Burundi	Imana
Cameroon	Njinyi, Nyooiy
Central African Republic	Nzapa, So, Mbori
Gabon	Anyame, Nzame
Ghana	Bore-Bore, Dzemawon, Mawu, Na'angmin, Nyame, Onyankopon
Botswana	Modimo, Urezhwa
Ethiopia	Arumgimis, Igziabher, Magano, Tel, Tsuossa, Waqa, Yere, Yere Siezi
Ivory Coast	Nyame, Onyankopon
Kenya	Akuj, Asis, Mulungu, Mungu, Ngai, Nyasaye, Tororut, Wele (Were)
Lesotho	Molimo (Modimo)
Liberia	Yala
Madagascar	Andriamanitra, Zanahary
Malawi	Cauta, Chiuta, Lexa, Mulungu, Unkurukuru, Utixo
Mozambique	Mulungu

Namibia	Kalunga, Mukuru, Ndjambi Karunga, Pamba
Nigeria	Ondo, Chuku, Hinegba, Olodumare, Olorun, Osanobua, Osowo, Owo, Soko
Rwanda	Imana
Sierra Leone	Leve, Meketa, Ngewo, Yatta
South Africa (Azania)	Inkosi, Khuzwane, Modimo, Mwari, Raluvhimba, Unkulunkulu, Utixo
Sudan	Ajok, Bel, Dyong, Elo, Jok (Juok, Juong), Kalo, Kwoth, Mbori (Mboli), Nhialic, Nguleso, Ngun Tamukujen
Swaziland	Mkulumncandi, Umkhulumncandi
Tanzania	Enkai, Ishwanga, Kyala, Kyumbi, Mulungu (Murungu), Mungo, Ruwa
Uganda	Akuj, Jok (Juok), Katonda, Kibumba, Ori, Rugaba, Ruhanga, Weri
Zaire	Akongo, Arebati, Djakomba, Katshonde, Kmvoum, Leza, Nzambi
Zambia	Chilenga, Chiuta, Lesa (Leza), Mulungu, Nyambe, Nzambi, Tilo
Zimbabwe	Unkulunkulu, Mwali (Mwari), Nyadenga

There are thousands of other names for God. Some are personal and mean only God, and others are descriptive, that is, they describe something about him. These names show us clearly that African peoples are very familiar with the belief in God, and that over the years they have formulated certain ideas about God. Some of the names, like Chiuta, Jok, Leza, Mulungu, Nyame, Nzambi and others, are commonly used in several African languages. This suggests that a long time ago, before these languages became separate, the names of God were already being used, and the belief in God had already become a major feature of African thinking and life.

In every African language and people, there is at least one personal name for God. Because these personal names are often very ancient, their meanings are no longer known, as we have said. On the other hand, descriptive names often have particular meanings, and in some languages there are up to ten or more such names for God. Thus, Africans are rich in their ideas about God, and many books have been and are being written about God as understood by African peoples. (A list of some of these books is given in Appendix B at the end of the book. They are advanced books and are mentioned here only for those readers who have the interest and educational background to do further reading on the subject of the African belief in God.)

African ideas about God can be grouped into four general categories. These are: what God does, human pictures of God, the nature of God, and people's relationship with God. In this chapter we shall look at the first three of these, and the final set of ideas will be dealt with separately in the next chapter.

• **What God Does**

African peoples believe that God does many things in the universe.

God is the Creator of all things

First and foremost God is said to be the Creator of all things. This belief is common everywhere in Africa. For that reason there are many names which describe him as Creator, Creator of all things, Moulder, Begetter, Bearer, Maker, Potter, Fashioner, Architect, Carpenter, Originator, Constructor, and so on. There are also hundreds of African myths which tell about God's work of creation.

Some African peoples say that God created the universe out of nothing. Others believe that he first created certain things, and then used their substance to create more things. God created when there was nothing, and he continues to create new things. He has never stopped his work of creation. He also continues to shape and reshape what he has created.

It is believed in some societies that when God was in the process of making all things, he made helpers or assistants whom he put in charge of making certain things under his supervision and direction. But in most African societies, people believe that God alone was responsible for making everything without a helper and without an assistant. What he made included the visible and invisible universe, the heavens and the things thereof, the earth and the things thereof. He also established the laws of nature to govern the world, and gave people laws, customs and gifts by means of which they could live.

God sustains his creation

God also sustains, keeps and upholds the things he has created. This means that he looks after the universe, cares for it and keeps

The baobab tree, featured in religious rites and myths.

Murchison's Falls on the River Nile in Uganda.

The Kenyan government burnt 12 tons of elephant tusks which had been confiscated from poachers, in Nairobi, on 17 July 1989.

it together, so that it does not fall apart or disintegrate. As a result of this belief, people speak of God as the Keeper, Upholder, Protector, Preserver, Guardian, Caretaker, Pastor and Saviour. For that reason they feel that the world and the universe have no end, and will never end, because God keeps them and sustains them. They also believe that even though individuals are born and die, human life as such has no ending since God is its Protector and Preserver.

God provides for what he has created

God provides for what he has created. This activity of God is commonly called Providence. It shows the goodness of God towards the whole universe. He provides life, sunshine, rain, water, good health, the fertility of people and animals and plants, food and protection. For that reason, African peoples call him the Giver of things, Water Giver, Healer, Helper, Guard, Source. They believe that God only gives good things. All African peoples pray, therefore, asking God to give them what they need and come to their rescue, because they believe that God provides.

God rules over the universe

God rules over the universe. In this aspect he has names like King, Governor, Ruler, Chief, Master, Lord, Judge and Distributor. In their prayers people acknowledge God to be the Ruler and Governor of the universe. The idea of God as King is commonly found among African peoples which have or had traditional rulers. For them God ruled the universe just as their chief or king ruled their country. To speak of God as the Ruler of the universe means that there is no spot which is not under his control; nothing can successfully rebel against him or run away from him.

It is strongly believed that God rules in perfect justice. Therefore he is also referred to as the Judge. People say that he judges all things justly, distributes all things justly, rescues the oppressed and punishes the wrongdoer. For this reason he is also called the Arbiter of the world. At times he punishes wickedness by means of sickness, disease, accident, famine, drought, storm, war, calamity or even death. Yet people may pray to him to forgive and take away punishment.

These then are some of the major activities of God as found in African Religion. Let us now see how people picture God in human terms.

• Human Images of God

Since God is considered to do the things we mentioned in the previous section, and since many of these activities are similar to those carried out by people, it is helpful to the imagination for people to picture God as if he has human characteristics. Such mental images are aids to our understanding of God; they illustrate something about God. It does not mean that God is looked on as a human being. These mental images have their limitations, but they nevertheless assist the mind to have a working knowledge of God. They also help people in communicating their ideas about God. Other human images make people feel close to God even though he is their Creator. It is because of such images that people can approach God, as we shall see in the next chapter.

Almost everything that people say about God is in the end a human picture or image, since they have to use human language, and language is made up of images and concepts. The names mentioned in the previous section which describe God as Maker, Potter, Architect, Helper, Giver, Protector, Pastor, King, Judge and so on carry human images which are transferred to God in order to clarify certain ideas about him. In addition there are other images, which we can mention here briefly.

God as Father, Mother or Parent

A number of African peoples look upon God as Father and themselves as his children. This image gives the idea of a family. It shows a close relationship between people and God. It implies that God has not only 'begotten' or made the people, but is also their protector, provider and keeper. In a few African societies, God is also regarded as the Mother of people. This idea is found in the societies whose social organisation is centred on the home and position of the mother. The point in both images is that God is the Parent and people are his children. In some places he is even called the Great Ancestor, the Elder, the Grandfather, meaning that it is from him that all people and all things originated.

The idea of God as Parent is also shown in prayers which people offer to him. The prayers are addressed to him in a manner similar to that of children speaking to their parents about themselves and their needs. People communicate with God in the same way that human children communicate with their parents. When in difficulties, people may call to him as 'Oh Father!', or 'My Father!' 'Our Father', 'Oh Mother!'

God as Friend

In some places, God is called Friend, or the Greatest of Friends. This is an image which shows great confidence in God. People feel at home with him, believing that he is trustworthy, faithful, close to them and ready to help them just as a true human friend would do. Because he is their Friend, they can speak to him or with him as freely as they wish. They know that he is always there for them.

Images of bodily parts of God

Another human image has to do with bodily parts attributed to God. People say that God sees, hears, smells, tastes. Others say that he has ears, eyes or wings. The sky, sun and moon are taken to be the eyes of God, that is, they symbolize God's ability to see. These symbols of God's eyes may have been suggested by the fact that the sky is full of lights both in the daytime and at night. When people refer to these objects as the eyes of God, they are speaking metaphorically to mean that God sees everything and everywhere. In fact one vivid name of God in Uganda means 'the Great Eye', which emphasizes God's ability to know all things.

Images of activities of God

There are other human activities said in different parts of Africa to be carried out by God. They include eating, sleeping, playing, walking, rejoicing, getting angry, speaking, thinking and remembering. All these are metaphorical ways of explaining how God is thought of in human terms, even though people do not mean to say that he literally does all those things or that he is a human being. By using such words about God, people are able to feel closer to him than would otherwise be the case. They can then sacrifice to him, make offerings to him, call upon him, cry to him, pray to him, invoke him and in many ways feel confident that he is truly their Maker, who is, at the same time, involved in their life.

• The Nature of God

In this section we ask questions like these: exactly who is God, what is he like, what makes him truly God? African peoples are agreed that nobody has seen God. Therefore nobody can really describe him. Yet, through their religious insights, they have formulated certain ideas about the nature of God. These ideas concern his real being, that which differentiates him from the things he has made.

God is good

In many parts of Africa, God is described as being good. He is not only the Maker of all things, but he is good towards all people and all things. People reach this conclusion from observing what he gives them, and how readily he may be approached. For example, some of the people of Zaire say, 'Rejoice, God never does wrong to people!' And in Liberia they say, 'God causes rain to pour down on our fields, and the sun to shine. Because we see these things of his, we say that he is good!' In Ghana people look at the works of God and proclaim, 'God is good, because he has never withdrawn from us the good things which he gave us!' There are many similar sayings all over Africa which show that people consider God to be absolutely good, and that his goodness never ends. He never gets tired of doing good, for he is the fountain of goodness.

God is merciful

It is widely believed that God is merciful and kind. Therefore people call him 'the God of pity', 'the Merciful One', 'the Kind One', and 'the God of mercy'. At other times they simply say, 'God is kind', and 'God is merciful'. In pronouncing blessings this expression is often used: 'May the God of mercy go (or remain) with you!' When special help has been received from God, people sometimes say, 'God had mercy on me!' or, 'If God had not shown mercy to me, I should be dead by now!' These sayings are used when someone has escaped from danger, misfortune or serious illness. The mercy and kindness of God are shown towards all his creation, especially people. He is the source of all mercy and kindness. Therefore people expect others to show kindness and mercy towards one another, and these qualities are highly appreciated in African societies. They come ultimately from God, even if people may not always show them in their behaviour towards one another.

God is holy

God is thought to be holy and pure. He cannot and does not do anything wrong or evil. He has no fault or failure. In Nigeria people speak of him as 'the Pure King', 'the King without blemish', and 'the Whiteness without patterns'. These vivid expressions describe an otherwise abstract idea of God's holiness. In Kenya some people speak of him as 'the Possessor of Whiteness', and associate him with the snowy top of Mount Kenya.

Because God is thought to be holy and without blemish, people everywhere are careful in making sacrifices to him. They conduct themselves properly, with reverence, fear, respect and honour towards him. Often the animals which are sacrificed to God have to be of only one colour, either white, black, brown or red. This is a symbolic way of saying that since God is pure and holy, he should be given holy or clean animals. Those who lead others in the rituals and ceremonies directed to God have to be men or women of moral integrity who have not committed murder or theft or adultery or anything evil in the sight of their community.

God is all-powerful

It is widely believed that God is all-powerful and almighty. This belief comes out in many ways and expressions. People say that God can do all things, or that there is nothing which God cannot do. But it must be remembered that he can only do what is good and right, and what is consistent with his own nature. In some African languages, we have names of God which speak of him as the All-Powerful, the Almighty, the Irresistible, the Powerful One, the Possessor (or Owner) of all strength, and so on. This same idea of God's powerfulness comes out in other expressions, as for example, when people say: 'It is only God who makes the sun rise and set', 'God can turn things upside-down', 'God thunders', 'Everything is possible with God', 'God is the Master of all things', or 'God roars so that all nations are struck with terror'. What man cannot do, God can do. Nobody would dare to oppose God, since all power, all strength, all might, belong to him. Because he created all things and governs all things, he must therefore be more mighty and more powerful than all that he has created. This is the logic that people follow in thinking about the power of God.

God is all-knowing

Another common belief about God is that he knows all things. There is nothing hidden from him. He is called the Wise One, whose wisdom, knowledge and understanding are without limit.

Therefore some people in Nigeria say: 'Only God is wise!' In order to show this idea more forcefully, people speak of God as the All-seeing and the All-hearing, the Watcher of everything, the All-seer, and the Discerner of hearts. These expressions mean that everything is within the reach of God's understanding and knowledge: it is as if he hears each and every sound, and sees each and every atom or particle of his vast creation. Some people say poetically that God is the Big Eye, and others that God has long ears. So the wisdom and knowledge of God penetrate into and through everything and nothing can be hidden from him.

God is present everywhere

God is simultaneously present everywhere in the universe. This belief is expressed in various ways among African peoples. For example, in some areas God is known as the Great Pool; other people say that God is everywhere at once; in Cameroon one of the names of God means 'He who is everywhere'; in Zambia some of the people say that God never comes to an end anywhere or at any time.

Often the wind or air is taken as a metaphor for speaking about God's presence everywhere. People say that he is like the air or like the wind. Just as they cannot get away from the air and live, neither can anyone run away from the presence of God. It is also because of this belief that people pray everywhere and at any time, where and when the need arises. Sometimes if a person harms someone else and hides it, people say that no matter how long he may hide it, God sees him and will deal with him accordingly.

It must be made clear, however, that even though God is everywhere simultaneously, he is not identical with anything or any place. There may often be places and moments where and when the presence of God is felt more than at other times and in other places. But this does not mean that he is more present there or then than elsewhere and at other times. For example, people may feel his presence more at a shrine or sacred grove, but he is neither that shrine nor that grove. People may feel his power in a thunderstorm, but he is not the thunder or the lightning which accompanies it. People's senses may focus upon God's presence at certain times of the day, month or year, or during certain of life's experiences, and in certain places, especially those associated with worship. This only means that God's presence may be found anywhere and at any time.

God is limitless

Although God is present everywhere, people also believe that he has no limit. He is both very far and very near, he is both beyond and within. There is neither time nor space beyond God, just as there is neither time nor space in which God is absent. This is a difficult idea to grasp, but African peoples seem to have thought it out. Some of them say, 'God is the Ancient of Days.' This means that he is 'older' than the oldest of the very first day in creation; therefore he is beyond time itself, and yet he is within time. In some places he is described as 'the Limitless One who fills all space'. In Sierra Leone, one of God's names means 'the High-up One'; while in Zambia he is called 'the Besetting One'. The first of these two names speaks about God's distance from all things, while the second name speaks about his nearness to all things. God is both simultaneously far away and very near. Thus, God cannot be exhausted by human imagination, and some people in Zaire even have a name for him which means 'the Unexplainable'.

God is self-existent

While God has made all things, he himself is not made. He exists on his own: he is self-existent. This idea is expressed by the Pygmies who say that 'God was the first who had always existed and will never die'. In South Africa some people have a name for God which means 'He who is of himself' or 'He who came into being of himself'. In other parts of Africa it is believed that God has neither father nor mother, and that he is neither a child nor an old man. So the question of how God originated does not arise; it is a meaningless question as far as he is concerned, nor is there an answer for it. God is not created, he is not begotten, he is not born, he is not made: he exists of his own, and from his own existence all things received their own existence.

God is the first cause

Another idea, connected with the previous one, is that God is the first and last cause. So he is called the Original Source, and the Beginning of all things. Other people call him simply the Beginner, and the First Great Cause. These ideas are well summarized in a traditional African hymn to God, used by the Pygmies in Zaire, which starts as follows:

In the beginning was God,
Today is God,
Tomorrow will be God . . .

God is spirit

Another belief about the nature of God is that he is spirit, invisible
and everlasting. For that reason some people call him simply the
Great Spirit, the Fathomless Spirit, the Ever-present Spirit, or the
God of Wind and Breath. The air or wind is often used as a
metaphor when speaking of God as spirit. People see or feel the
effect of the air, but they do not see the air or wind itself. So
people see, feel and know the effect of God in the universe even if
they do not see him.

God never changes

It is believed that God never changes. Some people in Kenya say
that God is the same today as he was yesterday, and the Pygmy
hymn we quoted above makes precisely the same point. In central
Africa there is a proverb that says, 'God never dies, only men do!'
In Zaire one of his names means 'He of many suns, the eternal
God'. This means that his time is beyond reckoning, he does not
change, he is not subject to the natural processes of growth, old
age, decay or death. In fact, in Nigeria the people sing that
'Nobody has ever heard about the death of God, because he never
dies!'

God is unknowable

Above all, it is believed that God cannot be explained, he cannot
be fully known. African peoples have long known this, and God
has names which mean 'the Unknown', 'the Unexplainable', 'the
Fathomless Spirit'. What the people of Zaire and Angola say about
God being the Marvel of Marvels, is a fine summary of African
belief about God everywhere. People know only very little about
God. The rest of his real nature remains a great mystery and a
great marvel. God is only God: no more, and no less.

6 · How God is Approached by People

• The Meaning and Purpose of Worship

In the previous chapter we saw that African peoples have a strong belief in God. One of the many ideas they hold about him is that God is everywhere and at all times. On the one hand he is greater than all the things he has made, while on the other hand he is so near that people can approach him. They believe that he pays attention to them. Certain ways of approaching God have, therefore, been developed in African societies. There are similar methods in other religions of the world. These ways of approaching God are often called worship. We shall first of all look at the meaning of worship, and then consider some of the methods of worship in African Religion.

In some African languages, there is no word for worship as such. Instead, we find other words like 'to pray', 'to sacrifice', 'to perform rituals', 'to make an offering', and so on. These words describe things and actions which are directed towards God and spiritual beings. Here we shall use the word 'worship' which includes all these actions.

Worship is a means of renewing contact between people and God, or between people and the invisible world. African people are very much aware of the existence of the invisible world, which they see as a real part of the universe. They perform acts of worship to keep alive the contact between the visible and invisible worlds, between men and God.

Worship is also used as a means of creating harmony in the world of mankind. People turn to God generally when trouble comes. They need at such times to restore their peace, happiness and sense of security. If nothing is done, they fear that things will get worse. Worship helps them to get back a sense of peace and religious harmony in their life and in the world at large.

Through worship, man cultivates a spiritual outlook on life. He reminds himself that he is both body and spirit, and that he needs to look after both of these in order to have full integrity. Without this spiritual direction or orientation, man would feel lost in the universe, and life would seem to have no meaning. We saw early in the book that according to African ideas, this is a deeply religious universe. Worship helps to implement that view.

Through worship, man exercises his position as the priest of the universe, the one who awakens the universe and links it with God its Creator.

Acts of worship are a means of linking the spiritual and physical worlds, putting the invisible into touch with the visible. Through worship man becomes the intelligent bridge between these two worlds, and between the Creator and the creation.

In many African societies it is told in myths that at the beginning God and man were in very close contact, and that the heavens (or sky) and the earth were united. For various reasons this link was broken and God became more distant from the people. But through worship man is able to restore that original link to a certain extent. Worship helps people to feel that there is still a relationship between God and man, and that communication between them is still possible. Worship brings them closer together, so that people are able to feel that they are the children of God. Worship creates a sense of friendship between God and people, since in worship it is man who strives to approach God. He does so in the belief that God is approachable.

Let us now look at the main African ways of approaching God through worship.

• Prayers

Prayer is the commonest method of approaching God. It is found in all African societies. People may pray privately, as individuals, or as heads of their families. Other prayers are made communally, at public meetings and for public needs. Anybody can pray to God at any time and in any place. But there are also people who generally pray on behalf of others. These include priests (both men and women), rain-makers, chiefs, kings, and sometimes medicine men, who may pray for the general public or for private individuals who ask their assistance. Within the family, praying is normally done by the head of the family or the oldest member of the family, but sometimes a ritual elder or local priest may be asked to do this.

African traditional prayers generally include praise, thanksgiving, a declaration of the state of affairs in which the prayers are offered, and requests. Such prayers always have concrete intentions, and people do not 'beat about the bush' when saying their prayers. They request such things as: good health, healing, protection from danger, safety in travelling or some other undertaking, security, prosperity, preservation of life, peace and various benefits for individuals. For the community at large, prayer may ask for rain, peace, the cessation of epidemics and dangers to the nation, success in war or raids, the acceptance of sacrifices and offerings, and fertility for people, animals and crops.

In prayers people sometimes express their gratitude to God for help given to them. They thank him for a safe journey or the delivery of a child, for long life, for many children, for prosperity, for preservation from danger and sickness, and so on. On a communal level, God may be thanked for giving rain, for driving away the enemy, for warding off epidemics or locusts, and for accepting sacrifices. People may also address praise and appreciation to God for his greatness, his kindness, and his readiness to listen to them, and for doing many things in their favour. African praise is often expressed in the descriptive names of God which are invoked during prayer, such as the God full of pity, the Saving Spirit, the Father of the placenta, the Ancient of Days, the Ruler and Giver of all things.

Many different prayers are used all over Africa. Some of them have been recorded in books, but many have not. People pray for different reasons and at different times. Some prayers have been used many times by past generations, and have become formal. They are often in poetical forms and can be readily memorized. But other prayers are offered according to the demands of the occasion. Some can be as short as two or three words, while others are much longer. People pray because they believe that God listens to them, accepts and answers their prayers. They also pray because they believe that he is near to them, since he is everywhere simultaneously. When people pray they may kneel, sit down, prostrate themselves, remain standing, or clap their hands and sing.

Let us take a few examples of prayers in African Religion. In Kenya, this prayer is said before someone goes to work: 'God, help me so that I do not see any danger while I work, because I know that there is danger all around!' In the Cameroon, a man who prays for his sick wife says, 'You alone, O God, ordained that we should marry women. Therefore grant that my wife, who is now sick, may recover speedily.' In Zaire, when there is danger of a storm, the following prayer would be said: 'Father, your children are in great anguish. Calm the tempest, for here live many of your children. Do you not see that we are dying?'

In praying, people are addressing themselves to the invisible world. They do not see God, but they believe that he is present with them. Prayer is an act of pouring out the soul of the individual or community. In praying, people get as close as they can to God, since they speak to him directly. Communal prayers also help to cement together the members of the group in one intention, for one purpose, and in one act of worship. Some communal prayers include choruses of litanies, which are spoken by the group in response to the direction of their leader. In this way, everyone takes part in the prayer, just as everyone shares in the need expressed in that prayer.

Thus, praying strengthens the links between man and God, and man and his fellow man. Prayers help to remove personal and communal anxieties, fears, frustrations, and worries. They also help to cultivate man's dependence on God and increase his spiritual outreach.

• Making Sacrifices and Offerings

The practice of making sacrifices and offerings is found all over Africa. By this practice material or physical things are given to God and other spiritual beings. This act marks the point where the visible and invisible worlds meet, and shows man's intention to project himself into the invisible world. People make sacrifices and offerings of almost any animal or object. The distinction between sacrifices and offerings is this: sacrifices involve the shedding of the blood of human beings, animals or birds; offerings do not involve blood but concern the giving of all other things, such as foodstuffs, water, milk, honey or money.

In African societies, life is closely associated with blood. When blood is shed in making a sacrifice, it means that human or animal life is being given back to God who is in fact the ultimate source of all life. Therefore the purpose of such a sacrifice must be a very serious one. Such sacrifices may be made when the lives of many people are in danger. The life of one person or animal, or of a few of either, is destroyed in the belief that this will save the life of many people. Thus, the destruction of one becomes the protection of many.

The kind of situation that calls for a sacrifice may include drought, epidemics, war, raids, calamity, insect pests, and destructive floods. Since these affect the community, it is the community which then sacrifices an animal or, in past years, a human being. Such animals are carefully chosen to make sure that

Sacred grove and shrine of the principal riverain divinity Oshun; there is a major festival for her (Nigeria).

Inside the shrine, showing the altar where sacrifices and prayers are made for the cure of barren women, peace and prosperity (Nigeria).

they are acceptable to God. Usually they have to be of one colour, which may be black, white, red or brown; and if they are domestic animals they have to come from an upright owner. Wild animals are also sacrificed. For personal and family needs, only animals are sacrificed. Such family needs may concern health, marriage problems, remembering the departed, or requests for prosperity or success. Usually domestic animals such as sheep, goats, cattle, dogs, or fowls are sacrificed, either by the family head or by the local ritual elder.

Offerings which, like sacrifices, are given for both communal and personal or family needs, include whatever people wish and are able to give. They can be both expensive and cheap, or even have no particular worth as such.

Communal sacrifices and offerings are normally made at shrines, or in sacred groves, or other holy places such as hills, lakes, waterfalls, and so on. Personal sacrifices and offerings are normally made in or near the home, and in some areas people have shrines in their homes for this purpose. They may also be made in public places of sacrifice, or as the ritual elder or diviner may direct.

A communal shrine, with pots used for offerings and libations (Nigeria).

Prayers always accompany offerings and sacrifices, so that the purpose of the sacrifice or offering may be declared. People feel that for important needs they should not approach God with empty hands. They know that God will not literally eat or make use of their sacrifice or offering. But they want to show their humbleness before him, the seriousness of their need, perhaps even their desperation. Sometimes the offerings and sacrifices are eaten by the ritual leaders. Sometimes they are shared out among those present. Sacrifices may also be left on the spot to be consumed by wild animals, or to rot away. In some cases, the offerings which have been blessed are then given back to their owners for normal use.

People make offerings and sacrifices in order to draw the attention of God to their needs, but these things are not always given to him directly. It is believed that God does not need such things. The sacrifices and offerings are then made to lesser spiritual beings, such as divinities, spirits and the departed. These act as go-betweens between men and God. They are expected to receive the offerings and sacrifices, and then relay people's requests to God. Yet most people do not concern themselves with such distinctions. As long as they have made a sacrifice or offering in accordance with the proper procedures, they are satisfied. The leader of the ceremony may know precisely to whom the sacrifice or offering is being given, but the rest of the participating crowd

Dancing as a popular expression of celebrating life and entertainment (Uganda).

A dancing group ready for action (Kenya).

may not always know or even care, as long as the ceremony is done properly.

• Singing and Dancing in Worship

When there is a communal act of worship in which prayers are offered, or sacrifices and offerings are made, this is often an occasion for singing, and dancing. Africans enjoy celebrating life. Therefore when people meet together for public worship they like to sing, dance, clap their hands and express their rejoicing. Some prayers have choruses and litanies which are said or sung by the group in response to the leader.

Some ceremonies of worship involve moving from one place to another. As they do this, people beat their drums, play musical instruments, dance and rejoice. Religious singing is often accompanied by clapping and dancing, which express people's feelings of joy, sorrow or thanksgiving.

Through music, singing and dancing, people are able to participate emotionally and physically in the act of worship. The music and dancing penetrate into the very being of the worshipping individuals. Some of the dancing and singing sessions which accompany communal worship may last the whole day or even several days. Afterwards people feel satisfied in spirit, even though tired in body.

• Intermediaries between God and Man

People feel themselves to be very small in the sight of God. In approaching him they sometimes need the help of someone else, just as in social life it is often the custom to approach someone of a high status through someone else. For that reason, some African peoples make use of helpers in approaching God, although they also approach him directly.

These helpers may be called intermediaries. Some are human beings, while others are spiritual beings. The human beings include priests, kings, medicine men, seers, oracles, diviners, rainmakers and ritual elders. These are often the ones who conduct acts of worship, whether formal or informal, and attend to the needs of their community. People go to them and tell them their needs, and it is then their duty to approach God through prayer, sacrifice, offerings and the interpretation of visions or dreams. We shall say more about them in a later chapter.

Among the spiritual beings who are believed to help people in their approach to God are divinities, some spirits, especially those of former national leaders and heroes, and those of the dead who are still remembered in the family. When people make prayers, sacrifices and offerings, they sometimes address members of their families who died recently. For national or communal needs, the people may address departed kings, chiefs, clan founders, or the divinity or spirit of the area.

The intermediaries are a link between God and the Creator and human beings. It is believed that they have easier access to him than ordinary people, although anybody can approach God directly if they have need to do so. The idea of intermediaries fits well with the African view of the universe, which holds that the invisible world has its own life and population. The life of this invisible world is in some ways higher than that of man, but God is higher still. In order to reach God effectively it may be useful to approach him by first approaching those who are lower than he is but higher than the ordinary person.

The notion of intermediaries also helps people to feel protected from the greatness of God which might otherwise crush the individual. People fear to come alone too close to God. By using intermediaries, they feel that someone speaks on their behalf, taking their message to God. In some places, the departed are regarded as intermediaries because it is felt that they speak both the language of the invisible world and the language of human beings. We call the departed of recent generations 'the living dead' and in some ways they form a link in the chain of contact between their living family members and the invisible God. People also feel that they are approaching God through someone who is known to them, who is part of them and shares the concerns and needs of the people.

Although African peoples use these intermediaries in performing some of their acts of worship, they do not worship the intermediaries themselves as such. They simply use them as conveyor belts, as helpers or assistants. By speaking through intermediaries they feel that they show more respect, esteem, honour and courtesy towards God, who must be approached with reverence and humility.

Thus, even though people are free to approach God directly, and often do so, they also feel the need for a bridge between them and their Creator. The intermediaries are not intended to cut God off from the people. They are windows and channels through which people may come closer to God. For some of the minor needs of life, people may find it more fitting not to trouble God, but prefer to address themselves only to the intermediaries.

It is through the various acts of worship described here that African Religion provides people with the feeling that God is close to them and they to him. People are not alone in the world, and God has not deserted them. They are able to approach him with a feeling of confidence and assurance. They believe that God cares for them, listens to them, protects them, provides for them, heals them, and meets their needs. In some societies, as we have said, people approach God in some few cases but not always through the help of intermediaries, while in others they do so directly and without assistance. In either case the important thing is for people to feel at ease, satisfied and happy as they practise their religion and go through life's experiences.

7 · The Spirits

• Types of Spirits

We have seen that, according to African views, the universe is composed of visible and invisible parts. It is commonly believed that, besides God and human beings there are other beings who populate the universe. These are the spirits. There are many types of spirits. God is their Creator, just as he is the Creator of all things. The spirits have a status between God and men, and are not identical with either. But people often speak about them in human terms, or treat them as though they had human characteristics such as thinking, speaking, intelligence and the possession of power which they can use as they will. Because the spirits are created by God, they are subordinate to him and dependent on him, and some of them may be used by God to do certain things.

The types of spirits in the universe can be shown in form of a diagram as follows:

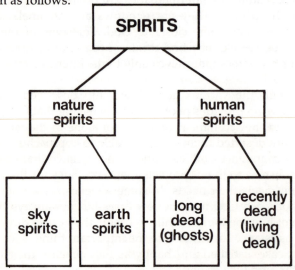

Although we can classify the spirits according to this diagram or in other ways, we have to bear in mind that they are all spirits. Therefore they have certain characteristics in common, just as peoples of different nationalities or races have common characteristics as well as differences.

• Nature Spirits

Nature spirits are those which people associate specifically with natural objects and forces. Some are thought to have been created by God initially as spirits; others are said to have been human beings of the distant past. The spirits propagate among themselves, and their population is on the increase.

Nature spirits are largely the personifications of natural objects and forces. This means that people give 'personal' characteristics to these objects and forces of the universe, regarding them as if they were living, intelligent beings of the invisible world.

Nature spirits of the sky

Some of the nature spirits are associated with objects and forces in the sky. These include: the sun, the moon, stars, 'falling stars', rainbows, rain, storms, wind, thunder and lightning. People say or believe either that such objects and forces are themselves the spirits, or that there are spirits occupying and controlling them.

In some African societies, it is believed that there are major spirits in charge of the stronger forces of the sky. These may be described as divinities or deities. They may be featured as ruling over, or being associated with the weather, storms, the sun, and so on. There are legends and myths about such divinities, their origin, their activities and their relationships with human beings.

Divinities are an important feature of African Religion in Nigeria, Ghana, Uganda and a few other countries. They and other sky spirits are mainly concerned with matters affecting large communities rather than single individuals. In some places, people make offerings and sacrifices to the divinities, asking them to help or relay their requests to God. At the same time people may also ignore them and approach God directly.

We should take note of three important points.

(i) There are many African peoples who do not believe that there are nature spirits in the sky at all. They see the heavenly objects or heavenly forces as direct works of God himself.

(ii) Even where Africans acknowledge the existence of these spirits, not all people pay attention to them by prayers, offerings and sacrifices. Nature spirits are looked on more as subjects for stories, myths and legends.

(iii) When people hold that there are spirits of the sky, such a belief helps them to explain the mysteries of the forces of nature connected with the sky, for which the people concerned have no

Symbols of the axe, mortar and human figures, for the divinity of thunder (Sango) (Nigeria).

other explanation. They explain such things in religious terms rather than in scientific terms, and they answer or ask different questions about nature. It satisfies the imagination of the people to accept the traditional view that thunder and lightning, for example, are caused by a spirit or divinity.

As scientific knowledge increases the people's understanding of these forces and objects of the universe, they will gradually give up the idea of nature spirits. But religion came long before science, and it will be a long time before rural communities are convinced by the spread of scientific ideas that there are no spirits behind the powers and forces of nature. Science looks on these phenomena as governed by natural laws; but religion may continue to think of them as ruled by spirits.

Nature spirits of the earth

Just as there are spirits associated with the things and forces of the sky, so there are those associated with the things and forces of the earth. These are the forces and things closest to human life. Therefore according to the beliefs of African peoples there are many such spirits. They are connected with: the earth, hills, mountains, rocks and boulders, trees and forests, metals, water in various forms (such as lakes, ponds, rivers, waterfalls and rapids,

A statue of the divinity Obatala, regarded to be the arch-divinity of the Yoruba and responsible for the primal creative activities of God (Olodumare) (Nigeria).

These Ancient rock paintings in a cave at Kavea (Kitui, Kenya), are estimated to be more than 3000 years old. The cave is used for offerings and sacrifices by the local people (Akamba).

lagoons and river banks), different animals and insects, certain diseases, and so on. As with the sky, these many things of the earth are thought to be occupied or moved by intelligent and living beings which are normally invisible to people. They are spoken of in human terms as if they can be pleased, offended, informed, interested, and so on.

Some of the nature spirits of the earth are of a higher status than others, and may be regarded as divinities. They may include, for example, the spirits of the sea, the lake and the forest. Diseases such as smallpox, and death itself, may be regarded as major spirits. This belief is commonly found in the same areas where objects and phenomena of the sky are regarded as divinities.

As there are so many possible objects and forces which may be associated with spirits of the earth, some are seen as more important than others in the lives of those who believe in them. In some places people may attribute spirits to forests, lakes, and rivers, but not to rocks and mountains. In other places, only certain diseases such as smallpox and lunacy may be associated with spirits, while the people concerned do not acknowledge other types of nature spirits.

The three points with which we ended the section on the spirits of the sky also apply to the nature spirits of the earth. Briefly they are: (i) not all African peoples believe that earth spirits exist; (ii) even those who recognize earth spirits do not all pay attention to them in form of offerings and prayers; and (iii) the idea of earth spirits provides people with a means of explaining many things that puzzle them in the world around.

Thus, through these nature spirits, African peoples have a direct link with both the inanimate things and forces of nature, and the living things. All these are seen from the point of view of man. This means that people project their own ideas on to these many things and forces of nature, and give them qualities and characteristics which resemble those of human beings. This makes sense to the people, and fits into the experiences of their life through the ages. People are not obliged to acknowledge any particular spirits all the time; they may abandon the idea of a particular spirit, if and when it does not look sensible or necessary. The spirits are, therefore, largely at the mercy of the people, even if by being invisible they may seem to defy the powers of human beings. People often ignore the spirits and look beyond to God both for his help and to explain the universe with its many mysteries.

• Human Spirits

Whereas nature spirits have no direct physical kinship with people, human spirits are those that once were ordinary men, women and children. Belief in the existence of these spirits is widespread throughout Africa. It is the natural consequence of the strong belief in African Religion that human life does not terminate at the death of the individual, but continues beyond death. It follows, therefore, that there must be myriads upon myriads of human spirits. Many of them appear in legends, myths and folk stories; others are spoken about in normal conversations among people; and some possess people, or appear to people in visions and dreams, or even in the open. We can think of human spirits as being of two different kinds.

Spirits of those who died a long time ago

There are countless numbers of these. Most of them are no longer remembered in their human form by anybody. People still believe that such spirits must exist in the invisible world. Some of them may be recollected through myths and legends as tribal, national or clan founders, and in reciting or recounting one's genealogies.

But the majority are spirits of forgotten people who are no longer within the personal memory of the living. People do not have clear ideas about these spirits of human beings who died in the distant past. It is thought that some of them have become nature spirits. Others may still be in the world of the departed (which is on this earth or underground and is very close to that of the living but invisible), while others are simply said to have disappeared into the unknown or to have vanished altogether.

When mentioned or featured in folk stories, the spirits of the distant past are sometimes presented in exaggerated human forms. In some stories they appear to be like animals or plants or inanimate things. They may be shown as doing both human and extra-human things, or they may appear stupid and naive. These spirits of folk stories are a literary device by means of which people caricature human life, satirize one another, make comments on society, and give an outlet to their feelings of fear, hatred or frustration without the danger of offending anybody. We see, therefore, that the idea of these spirits serves an important social and psychological purpose through the literary form. The idea of nature spirits helps to explain the mysteries of nature; the idea of human spirits helps to give outlet to people's emotions without their offending one another.

School children said to be in a state of 'spirit possession' (Akaba) (Kenya, 1985).

The spirits of people who were once leaders, heroes, warriors, clan founders and other outstanding men and women sometimes continue to be respected, honoured and brought into the life of the clan, community or nation. This is done through mythological legends about them and through ceremonies in which they feature. In some societies a few of the most outstanding spirits of the dead are elevated in mythology and ritual to the status of divinities, and may even be pictured as being close to God. The people ask for their aid through prayer and ceremony, or mention them when making their requests to God.

On the whole, people fear and dislike the spirits of those who died a long time ago, or of unknown persons, apart from those of the outstanding people mentioned in the previous paragraph. Another word for these spirits is ghosts. People fear them mainly because they are spirits of the unknown, and are therefore strangers to the living. People are not sure what might be done to them by such spirits. It is also believed that some of them may possess human beings, either voluntarily or without the wish of the people so possessed. Some diseases, such as meningitis, lunacy, and the condition of being deaf and dumb, are associated with spirits of this kind in some societies. On the other hand, diviners and medicine men are said to obtain some of their knowledge and insights from spirits. Thus, these spirits are not as completely bad as people may fear or say. Sometimes they act in unpleasant ways towards people, and sometimes in beneficial ways.

Spirits of people who died recently

People who died recently are remembered by their families, relatives and friends for up to four or five generations. We call their spirits the living dead, to distinguish them from the ghosts of those who died long before that. The belief in the existence of the living dead is widespread all over Africa, although it is held more strongly in some societies than in others. We will return to this topic later when we talk about remembering the departed and about the hereafter.

The living dead are the spirits that normally matter most on the family level. They are considered to be still part of their families. They are believed to live close to their homes where they lived when they were human beings. They show interest in their surviving families, and in return their families remember them by

A wooden carving showing imaginary spirits of the dead (husband and wife); the horn shape on their heads symbolises their profession as medicine men while they were human beings (Tanzania) (Left).

Wooden carving depicting an imaginary shape of a spirit (Kenya). Spirits of people long dead, or those connected with natural objects, are said to take on different shapes and forms (Right).

pouring out parts of their drinks and leaving bits of food for them from time to time. The living dead may also visit their surviving relatives in dreams or visions, or even openly, and make their wishes known.

When people face sickness and misfortune in the family, the cause may be attributed to the living dead, unless magic or sorcery and witchcraft are held responsible. In this case, these spirits serve as an explanation of what has caused things to go wrong. In order to put them right the spirits have to be satisfied by the performance of rituals, by following their requests, or by correcting any breaches of the proper conduct towards them. Generally the diviner or medicine man is consulted in order to find out exactly what the alleged spirits may wish. But on the whole the spirits of those who died recently are benevolent towards their families as long as they are remembered and properly treated.

People feel more at home with the spirits of the recent dead than with any of the other spirits. They are still very close to their surviving relatives, in both the memory and the emotions.

• What do Spirits do to People?

We may answer this question together with another one which asks whether spirits are evil or good, malevolent or benevolent. In fact, the majority of the spirits cannot be classified as either good or bad. Whether they are felt as good or bad depends on how people experience the forces of nature (in effect the nature spirits) and how they act towards human beings. The spirits can do both good and evil to people, just as people do both good and evil to their fellow human beings.

Spirits do not have concrete shapes and features, since by definition they have no physical form. But it is believed that when they appear to people, they may look like human beings, animals, insects or other things, and they can change suddenly to a different form. The spirits of the living dead look as they did when they were human beings. In telling about the spirits in folk stories, people tend to describe them in exaggerated forms. They say, for example, that they have enormous stomachs, that they can move or do other things extremely fast, that they readily find out secrets, that they combine a human face with an animal body, and so on. People draw and paint pictures or make carvings of their idea of spirits; or spirits are represented by masks at ceremonies and festivals (see pages 72, 73, 78, 133, 142). By bringing spirits so much into oral literature, art forms and ceremonies, people familiarize themselves with the spirits and therefore remove much of the fear that they might otherwise feel for these invisible and ubiquitous beings.

There are some societies, however, in which it is believed that certain spirits are wholly responsible for some of the evils that people experience in the world. Such spirits have become the scapegoats for people's troubles, even if other explanations may be forthcoming. These wholly wicked spirits are nearly always associated with death, and death itself is often regarded as a spirit.

The control of evil spirits

While in some societies it is believed that the spirits are innumerable and ubiquitous, it is always believed that God is above them all and keeps them under his control. If any spirit becomes bothersome to people, they may try to chase it away, get rid of it, or keep it at a distance; or they may appeal to God for help. Therefore, in the long run, people have the means of overcoming any mischievous spirits.

We have mentioned that some spirits help diviners, mediums, oracles and medicine men in their work. These are consulted as the need may arise. They are more or less the tools of their users. On the other hand the spirits that cause misfortunes, sickness, and even death may be used to do these things by human beings who have the power to do so, most often by witches, sorcerers or bad magicians. Thus, it is really people who use these spirits to do harm to their fellow human beings.

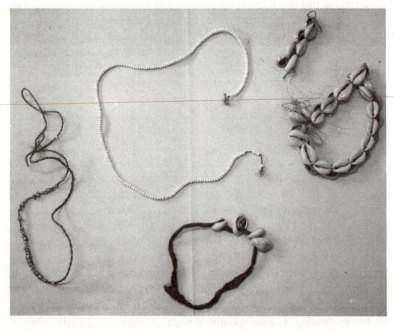

Articles used as necklaces and head-bands for a spirit cult (emandwa) (Uganda).

• Belief in Spirits Helps to Explain the Universe

We should remind ourselves that the belief in the existence of spirits provides people with the explanation of many mysteries which they find in the universe. This could be considered as a major benefit to people, where no other explanations are available or satisfactory. In the African view of the universe, the spirits fill up the area between God and man. This too can be a beneficial contribution to people's understanding of their own existence and that of God and the universe at large.

Whatever the spirits may do to people, and whatever people may do to the spirits, African Religion would have impoverished its followers if it had given no place to nature spirits and human spirits. Both seem to have been necessary and logical in the thinking and experiences of African peoples. What people in the past found meaningful through the idea of the spirits may today and tomorrow be found meaningful only through a different set of ideas. The fact remains, nevertheless, that the spirits are an integral part of the religious heritage of Africa. People are deeply aware of the spirit world, and this awareness affects their outlook and experiences in life for better and for worse.

At the funeral of Kabaka (King) Mutesa II in 1971, his body was laid to rest in the royal tomb, accompanied by traditional, state and Church rituals (Uganda).

81

8 · The Origin and Early State of Man

• The Value of Myths

Exactly when man came into being is unknown. Science has its own ideas, and religion has its own ideas. According to traditional African views, man was created by God. There are many myths and stories all over Africa which tell about the creation of man. Practically every African people has its own myths about it. Some of these myths differ considerably from people to people while others are remarkably similar across the continent. We can, however, put the ideas together and construct a general picture which emerges from a consideration of these myths and beliefs about the origin of man.

Since African peoples consider the universe to be centred on man, it is to be expected that there would be more myths about man's own origin and early state than about anything else. And this is indeed the case. A myth is a means of explaining some actual or imaginary reality which is not adequately understood and so cannot be explained through normal description. Myths do not have to be taken literally, since they are not synonymous with facts. They are intended to communicate and form the basis for a working explanation about something. In societies without written records of ideas and events, myths are often the most effective means of keeping ideas circulating from one place to another and from one generation to the next. Therefore African peoples have thousands of myths covering many themes and ideas. These myths are not only oral. Some are carved on wood, clay, ivory and stone; some are represented in arts and crafts; and others are retained in dances, rituals and ceremonies.

Obviously some myths are more important and meaningful than others; and some have a longer history than others. Myths continue to be formulated all the time. Because of the long history behind some of the myths, a study of African myths takes us back to the ideas, beliefs and experiences of people who lived on our continent many hundreds and thousands of years ago. Through myths we are able to dig deep into the psychology of the human past. We should not, therefore, lightly dismiss the value and significance of myths, even if we realize that they vary in importance and duration.

There are myths about God, about the creation of the universe, about the origin of man, about human institutions and values, about the coming of death, about heroes and leaders, kings and chiefs, animals and inanimate things. There are myths about natural forces and objects, about various habits of living and the behaviour of things around us. There are myths to answer the 'how', 'where' and 'why' questions which people have raised concerning the universe as a whole and man's immediate life in particular. Thus, in myths there lies a rich wealth of African ideas, beliefs, values, literary expressions and the exercise of human imagination.

• The Creation of Man

We can now look at the myths that describe the creation of man. They do not give us a literal picture of the origin of man. They show us explanation of the origin of man as people have thought about it. These explanations satisfied them and were passed on from generation to generation. The explanations also fitted satisfactorily into people's overall view of the world. Therefore these explanations of our forefathers should be received in the context in which they were formulated. They harmonized with people's other ideas and beliefs, giving them a complete and total picture of the world as they saw and experienced it.

Men from the sky

According to some myths, the first human beings were created in the sky or heaven, and then lowered to the earth. They were both husband and wife, and some peoples say that they were in two pairs so that the children from each pair were able to intermarry. Myths of this kind are found in Nigeria, the Sudan, Kenya, Uganda, Zambia and elsewhere. In some versions of the same idea, it is told that these first ancestors were thrown out of the sky (or heaven) to the earth as a punishment for doing wrong things. Other versions say that they were deliberately sent to the earth by God for the purpose of inhabiting it.

Men from the ground

The majority of creation myths tell about God creating men on this earth. There are many versions of how this was done. In some societies it is believed that God used clay to make the first man and wife. This idea is found in many parts of Africa. For that reason God has the name of Potter or Moulder in many areas. The details of how he used clay to make men vary from place to place, but the idea is generally the same.

In other myths it is said that God made the first man and woman in water or marshes, and then pulled them out, or let them come out themselves on to the dry ground. A related set of myths tells that God made people inside the ground, and let them out of a hole in the ground or in a rock. Both types of myth are found in eastern and southern Africa.

In some places it is believed that the first men fell off a tree like fruit. In Namibia this mythical tree is called 'the tree of life', and it is said to be situated underneath the ground. The myths which associate the creation of men with trees are spread across central Africa, the Sudan, parts of Zaire and elsewhere. Related to this idea is another set of myths which say that God made the first people and put them in a vessel which burst open or was opened by other creatures of God, and out came the people.

There are many other myths which cannot be considered here. Whatever the story may be, the ideas are that: (i) man was created by God; (ii) in almost every case it was either husband and wife, or two pairs; (iii) the creation of man took place generally at the end of the creation of other things. This last point may indicate that people believe that man was the completion or perfection of God's work of creation, since nothing else better than man was created afterwards. In some myths God is pictured as creating man without any assistance from what he had already created; but in others it is said that God used the help of some of the other creatures, either spirits or animals, but these acted under God's direction.

• The Condition of the First Men

Concerning the condition of the first men there are many ideas in the different myths of African peoples. We have seen in most cases, that they were male and female, in one or two pairs. This was to ensure that they would propagate and bear children. But in many myths it is said that the man and wife were originally ignorant of many things, including the question of bearing children. Only little by little did they learn various skills and ways of survival.

It is said in almost all the myths of man's creation that at first God was very close to men. He was the parent to them and they were his children. He supplied them with all the things they needed, like food, shelter and the knowledge of how to live. In some stories it is said that God supplied them with cattle, or other domestic animals, fire and implements for hunting, fishing or cultivating the land. God allowed or told them to do certain things but forbade other things.

The myths that describe the first men also usually say that people were intended to live forever. For this purpose God gave them one or more of three major gifts. One was the gift of immortality, which meant that death could not touch them at all. Another was the gift of becoming young again after getting old. The third was the gift of resurrection, which meant that even if death did kill people they would rise again. For various reasons these precious gifts were eventually lost, and men began to die and vanish forever. In a later chapter we shall consider the myths of how death came into the world.

The separation of God from men

In some myths it is told that at the creation of the first men, heaven and earth were joined by a ladder, rope or road, or were one substance. Therefore there was direct contact between the two parts of the universe. Since African peoples believe that the heavens are populated, it meant that the first men were in direct contact with the 'people' of the sky. Later this link was severed: the sky went up, the earth remained beneath. The separation of heaven and earth also resulted in the separation of God from men.

The separation of God from men is described in many myths all over Africa. In some places it is told that when people were pounding their food with mortar and pestle, they continually hit the nearer part of the sky, thereby irritating God. Therefore, he went up higher so that they would no longer reach him with their pestle. We hear this myth told in Ghana and other parts of western Africa. Another kind of myth says that the first people set fire to the grassland, and the smoke from this fire drove God away. This myth is found in the central African region.

Among the peoples of the Nile Valley in Uganda and the Sudan, the separation of heaven and earth is said to have come when the rope linking the two worlds was accidentally broken or eaten by the hyena. This animal seems to be unusually hungry, since it still roams about the countryside eating whatever it can. (Apparently the leather rope that once united the world below and the world above does not seem to have filled up its empty stomach!)

Many myths say that the separation came as a result of the first men breaking one of God's regulations. The regulation concerned varies from people to people. Some say that people were forbidden to eat eggs, to eat animals, to eat certain fruit or yam, or to fight with one another. On breaking this regulation, men were sent away or God withdrew from them, and they lost many of the original benefits that they once received from God.

The loss of the original paradise

All these many myths about the creation of men say that even though they were largely in a state of ignorance, they lived in a paradise at the beginning. God was close to them and gave them all that they needed. They were meant to live forever. The heavenly and earthly worlds were joined or close together, this being the symbol of harmony and tranquility. But this state did not last very long. For various reasons the original paradise was lost: men's direct link with God was severed or eclipsed, the closeness between the heavens and the earth was replaced by a vast gap without a bridge, the gifts of immortality and resurrection melted away, and death, disease and disharmony came and have reigned ever since. In short, paradise became a thing of the distant past, and African Religion has never been able to show men how to regain paradise.

This was a severe loss and blow to mankind. But life did not become altogether hopeless. There are many myths which go on to tell us how God made other provisions for men to live and cope with their new situations. He taught them new skills and knowledge and new codes of behaviour, and gave them leaders who would direct them in the complexities of life. These included teachers, kings and chiefs, queens, priests, seers, medicine men, diviners, strong men, national and clan founders, and so on. Through religion people are still able to approach God. Through marriage and childbearing, they are still able to achieve something of the original immortality; and when they die, it is believed that their spirits continue to survive even if there is no special bliss for them in the hereafter.

Thus, men lost much but they also began to adjust to their loss. Life has still some meaning at different stages between birth and death, for the individual and for the community, without their having to go back to the original paradise of man's creation. Our book will now take us from the myths of men's distant past to the realities of their daily life.

9 · Birth and Time of Youth

• A Child is Expected

People do not spend their energies regretting what happened after the creation of the first men. The lost paradise was not the end of everything. We saw in the previous chapter that God helped men to put up with their new situation, and to adjust to living in this world as it is. In the course of time, African peoples concentrated their attention on life's journey from before birth to after death. They wanted that journey to be meaningful, happy, safe and satisfactory. African Religion tries to make the journey of life worthwhile for both the individual and the community of which he is an integral part. We shall trace the steps of this journey, looking at the key points as they have been marked out by African peoples.

There is great joy when a wife finds out that she is expecting a baby. The arrival of a child in the family is one of the greatest blessings of life. African peoples greet this event with joy and satisfaction. The pregnant woman informs her husband, and before long other people get to know about it. Immediately steps begin to be taken to ensure the safety of the baby and mother during and after pregnancy. It normally takes nine calendar months for a human baby to be born, but in traditional African societies women calculate the period in lunar months, which come to about ten months or less. Pregnancy is a joyful period for the woman and her family. If it is the first pregnancy for her, it assures everyone that she is able to bear children. Once that is known, her marriage is largely secure, and the relatives treat her with greater respect than before.

Ways of assuring a safe birth

The pregnant woman has to observe certain regulations and taboos in order that all may go well with her and the baby. These vary from people to people. In some societies she stops sleeping with her husband altogether until several months after delivery, or even until after weaning the child (which may take one to two years). In some areas she is not allowed to do certain types of work like cutting firewood, using knives, drawing water, and so on. Other traditions may forbid her to eat foods thought harmful,

A wood carving showing the glory of motherhood and procreation (Sudan).

Oromo women perform a 'birth ritual' by singing and beating the skin from a fertile cow (Ethiopia).

such as meat from animals killed with poisoned arrows, salt and certain fats.

Some peoples perform rituals and make offerings to thank God for the expected child and to pray for the safety of the child and mother. For example, when a Pygmy woman discovers that she is expecting a child, she offers a portion of food to God and thanks him for the baby.

It is a common practice for the expectant mother to wear charms which are believed to protect her and her baby from harm. In some societies, the wife returns to her parents' home to await the delivery of her baby, especially if it is the first.

Should the expectant mother begin to have pregnancy complications the medicine man or diviner is immediately consulted to find out the cause and take the necessary measures to cure the trouble or prevent it from recurring.

Thus all possible care is taken during pregnancy to protect and safeguard the mother and the baby. Great shame falls on anyone who shows no respect to a pregnant woman, who beats her, or does anything harmful to her whether by word or by deed. She carries two lives, and these lives deserve double consideration and care.

• The Baby Arrives

In traditional African villages, there are always women who are called upon to act as midwives when the time for delivery arrives. Some are very experienced and may have assisted in the delivery of up to fifty or more babies in their area. Customs vary concerning what is done on the arrival of the baby. In some countries the expectant mother has to return to her parents to give birth at their home. In other places there are special houses put aside or erected for the occasion. All over Africa, men may not be present in the same house where delivery is taking place, unless there are exceptional reasons. Women are, therefore, the chief witnesses of the arrival of babies.

In some societies the woman stands up to give birth; in others she sits down; and elsewhere she lies down. There are also some places where she has to deliver the baby all by herself. The sex of the baby is announced through various methods, such as shouts or screams by the mother or other women attending her. People are always eager to know whether a boy or a girl has been born.

After the birth

When the baby has been born, the placenta is, in some societies, thrown into a running stream or dried up and kept for later rituals, while in others it is buried nearby or in the fields. People look upon the placenta as a religious link between baby and mother. Therefore its disposal is accompanied by rituals in many places. In the same way, the umbilical cord is disposed of ceremoniously, and in some areas such as Uganda it is dried up and kept for a long time with great care.

Throughout Africa there are many traditions concerning what is to be done with the baby and mother following childbirth. Ceremonies and rituals are performed to mark the occasion. These rituals are for purification, protection and thanksgiving purposes. It is held in many parts of the continent that childbirth is in some sense an impurity, which is then cleansed by rituals. At the same time, the purification ritual prepares the mother for the birth of the next child, so that there is no obstacle to the flow of life.

Other rituals are performed to give protection to the baby as it begins its long journey in life, to bring good fortune to it, to commit it to God for his care. It is believed that the child needs protection against magic, sorcery, witchcraft, the evil eye, disease, malicious spirits, and any other source of harm. This ritual of

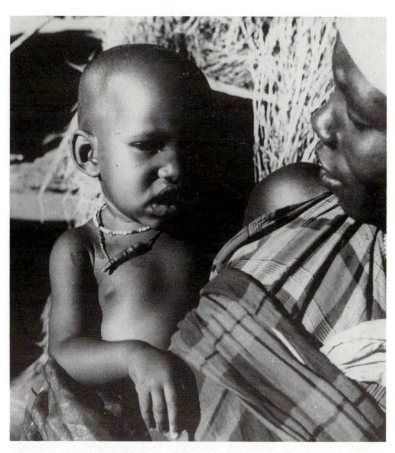

Child wearing protective medicine round the neck (Kenya).

protection is generally performed by the local medicine man or diviner, who also performs the purification ceremony. In many cases something is tied round the neck, waist or arm of the baby, as a physical sign of protection. One often sees such protective objects on babies and children in the villages, although these days they tend to be covered up with clothes.

Another intention of the ceremonies is to offer thanks to God for the safe arrival of the baby, and to pray for his continued blessings. Here is one such prayer from Kenya at the birth of a baby: 'O Creator who creates all human beings, You have given us a great worth, by bringing us this little child!' In this and similar prayers, people recognize that children are created by God and then given to them. For that reason he is called the Giver of Children and the Owner of People.

Introduction to society

There are many parts of Africa where, following the birth of a baby, both mother and baby (or just the baby alone) are kept in seclusion inside the house for several days. This is to give the mother time to rest and recover, and to allow the preparations for the ceremonies and festivals to be carried out. At the end of that period of seclusion, a large gathering of relatives, friends and neighbours is invited. Then in great jubilation the baby and mother are brought out of seclusion to be introduced to their family, relatives and friends. This is like a social birth for them: they now come out into the open to be received by society. In some places it is believed that even the living dead are also present for the occasion. In other areas the baby is introduced to the moon, to the sun or to God, in a short ceremony.

At the occasion of introducing the child to society, the baby's hair is often shaved. This is a sign of purification, separation and newness. It shows that anything bad is cut off, since it is shaved away with the old hairs. It also shows that the baby is now separated from the mother's womb, so that from that moment onwards it belongs to the whole family and the whole community. The shaving is a sign of newness, because the baby will now grow new hair as it enters a new phase of life. Symbolic washing also accompanies the ceremony, emphasizing purification.

Feasting, eating, dancing, rejoicing and congratulations to the mother and family follow. The whole occasion is a renewal of the life of the community. A new rhythm begins for everyone who participates in the ceremonies marking the birth of a baby. Now it is up to the community to integrate the baby into its life.

• The Baby is Given a Name

There are many naming customs all over Africa. In some places the name is chosen before the arrival of the baby; in others it is given immediately upon arrival and without any ritual or ceremony. But in most cases there is a naming ceremony, attended by members of the family, relatives, neighbours and friends. The name is considered in African societies to be very much part of the personality of the person. Therefore it is taken seriously, and chosen with care and consideration. Often names of people have a meaning, and it is this meaning which must be given due consideration.

The name can be chosen to mean various things. In some places, the baby is given the name of a departed relative whom the baby is considered to resemble closely. This makes people happy that a departed member of the family has 'come back' in part through the birth of the baby. This is a common belief in many parts of Africa. In other places, the baby is given the name of the day of the week on which it was born. This custom is followed in Uganda, Ghana and other parts of West Africa.

Names reflecting the feelings of parents

More often, however, the names chosen indicate the feelings of the parents and mark the occasion of the child's birth. When a child is born after many years of marriage, its name may indicate that God showed mercy or heard the prayers of the parents, or that people waited long for it, and so on. If the parents quarrelled during the pregnancy, the child's name may indicate this. The name may show that the first child or children died in infancy before the arrival of the one who has now survived. The name chosen would thus reflect the parents' gratitude to God for sparing this one, or it may be a name which speaks of the child as 'an ugly thing', or as 'an animal'. Animal names are often given for this purpose. The idea is that people have little hope that the child will survive, seeing that those born before it died; therefore they use animal or ugly names as a way of pretending that it is of little account, so that it will be allowed to survive. That is a form of prayer in desperation. (My own name, Mbiti, belongs to this category).

Names relating to the time of birth

The state of the weather is often reflected in people's names. Some are named after thunder, rain, drought, famine, harvest, weeding, hunting, and other seasons of the year. The events prevailing at the time of birth are also recorded in names referring to travelling, warfare, the arrival of Europeans, the establishing of a new school or church in an area, an invasion of locusts, promotion in a job or success in business, and so on.

Names that show religious feelings

Many of the names that are given show people's religious feelings. This practice is found all over Africa. We need to remember here that the feelings of people are very strong at certain stages of life, especially birth, marriage and death. Therefore it is no wonder that many African names reflect the religious feelings of the parents concerned. In some countries such as Burundi, Rwanda, Uganda and the Sudan, the name of God is often made part of the child's name. This shows how much people associate God with the continuation of life and the birth of children. Thus, for example, we have names like: *Byakatonda*, which means 'for or by the Creator' (*Bya + Katonda* – the second word is one of the names for God in Uganda); *Byaruhanga*, which means 'things of or for God' (*Bya + Ruhanga*, the last being a name for God in Uganda); *Bizimana*, which means 'God knows everything' (*Bizi + Imana*, the last being a name for God in Rwanda and Burundi), and many others. This custom has continued even under Christian influence, and many new religious names are being added which make use of Christian ideas without necessarily being borrowed foreign names. Thus, for example, we have names like *Tukacungurwaruhanga*, meaning 'We were saved by God' (*Ruhanga* being the name for God in parts of Uganda); *Asimwe*, meaning 'Let him (God) be thanked', and so on. African Christians and Muslims have adopted the custom of using religious names from their faiths and sacred books. In so doing, they are following the world-wide custom of using religious names, which is practised by Christians, Muslims and African traditionalists alike. This is an ancient and universal practice.

Names which describe the child or its background

There are names which mark the habits of the child, activities in the family or country, unusual events, the places where the child was born, the interests of the parents or community (such as keeping cattle, collecting honey, and trapping birds), relationships (especially names of kinsmen such as uncle, grandparents, nephew, and so on), economic life (such as riches, poverty or hardship), and many others. Children are usually given more than one name, though the rest are generally added as time goes by.

African names of people can tell a lot about their life. Some names may only be used by certain individuals; others are abandoned later, especially after initiation in some parts of Africa; and there are names of status, men's or women's associations, comradeship, and names for indicating when a person gets married, praising someone, old age and so on. Other names keep being added to a person as he (she) grows older, some are chosen by other people and some by himself. There is no end to giving names to people in African societies. But the most important occasion for the individual is at the very beginning when he receives the first name(s), although in some places later names may be given ceremoniously.

• When Twins and Triplets are Born

Approximately one out of every 80 births produces twins, and one out of every 6,400 births produces triplets. There are also other multiple births, but these are even rarer. Because these are unusual births, African peoples on the whole have given special attention to twins, triplets and other multiple births. In some places in the past, twins were considered to be a sign of misfortune, and one or both would be killed, or the mother would be killed. In other parts of Africa, the twins would be allowed to live, but people regarded them as having special powers from God. In either case, special ceremonies would be performed either to prevent the misfortune from happening again, or to activate the special powers of the twins, so that they would bring blessings to their people and community. In some parts of Uganda, for example, the umbilical cord of twins is valued enormously and may be kept for many years and used in ceremonies.

One reason why twins were disliked in some parts of Africa is that their chances of survival are generally less than those of single births; and the chances of survival for triplets are even less. In practice the twins and triplets died more often in infancy than did babies of single births. Therefore people were shocked when twins or triplets were born, and everyone feared that they would die, which often happened. The frequency of such deaths must have created the belief that it was unfortunate or abnormal to get twins or triplets. People did what they could in order to cleanse the supposed misfortune from spoiling the life of the community.

On the other hand, when twins or triplets survived in spite of the chances of their survival being much less than for single births, people felt that there was some power in them to make them survive. In turn this led to the belief that twins or triplets brought blessings to the family and community concerned. To acknowledge that belief, people tended to treat them with special consideration and to attribute much power to them.

Ceremonies and names marking the birth of twins and triplets are generally different from those of the ordinary single births. With increasing medical care all over Africa today, more and more twins and multiple births survive. Such children are as normal as any others, and there is no reason to fear them or regard them as having more power than other people.

• Growth, Circumcision and Initiation

It is the custom in African societies for the mother to breast-feed her baby. If she is not present, or if she does not produce enough milk, another woman with milk will normally feed the baby. Failing this, the baby is given goat's or cow's milk, in areas where these animals are kept. As the baby grows, it is introduced to other foods, starting with liquid or soft foods like porridge, fruit juice and pre-chewed food.

The appearance of teeth is greeted with some form of ritual in some parts of Africa. It is regarded as a misfortune if the baby gets the upper teeth before the lower teeth. The fact that this is unusual causes people to feel disturbed, wondering whether the event may herald further unusual events, which could be dangerous to the child and the community.

It may be up to two years before the child is weaned in some African societies. If in the course of that time the mother becomes pregnant again, the flow of milk usually stops, and weaning takes place earlier. In some parts of Africa children of the age to be weaned, or a bit older, are taken to stay with relatives for some time (which may be several months).

Generally no particular ceremonies or rituals are performed after those that mark the birth and naming of the child, until he is much older. In some parts, boys are circumcised at a very early age (even a few days after birth). In most cases, however, this is left until the period of puberty and after.

The second major point in the life of the individual comes when the young person goes through the initiation period. Not all African peoples mark this period with outstanding ceremonies, but most of them give it a special recognition. During that period a person goes through physical, emotional and psychological changes, which take him from childhood to adolescence and adulthood. This is a radical change for the individual concerned.

At a circumcision cermony, a boy is having his head shaved by his sister. The shaving symbolizes a ritual re-birth into a new stage of life (Tanzania).

One of the main initiation rites is that of circumcision for boys and clitoridectomy for girls. This is practised in many parts of Africa and is highly treasured in traditional life. Circumcision involves cutting off the foreskin of the boy's male organ; while clitoridectomy involves cutting some portion of the girl's female organ. In both cases, blood is spilt, and the operation is very painful, since often no pain-killing herbs or other preparations are used. Where the custom is followed, everyone must undergo it, for without it a person is still considered to be a child, no matter how old he or she might be, and it is shameful to be isolated from one's age-mates through lack of this experience.

In some parts of Africa, this form of initiation takes place annually, while in other parts it is a biennial event or even less frequent. It is also very much a community and public affair. Therefore the whole community makes a great occasion out of it. All the necessary preparations are carried out, the boys and girls due for the initiation are told in good time, everyone talks about it and waits for it with joy. The actual cutting of the skin is performed by qualified operators, and normally this is done to boys or girls in batches. Female operators do it on girls, and male operators on boys.

Some details vary from people to people, such as the age when initiation is done, who carries out the operation, at what time of year it is best done, where it is carried out, the type of preparation necessary for the boys and girls concerned, and the feasting which follows the great event. In many parts of Africa, the initiated youths are taken into seclusion in the woods for periods lasting from a few days to several months, or even longer in some cases.

• The Meaning and Importance of Initiation

What does initiation really mean and why is it so important in African life? There are many points in answer to this question.

A bond is made by the shedding of blood

The blood which is shed during the physical operation binds the person to the land and consequently to the departed members of his society. It says that the individual is alive, and that he or she now wishes to be tied to the community and people, among whom he or she has been born as a child. This circumcision blood is like making a convenant, or a solemn agreement, between the individual and his people. Until the individual has gone through the operation, he is still an outsider. Once he has shed his blood, he joins the stream of his people, he becomes truly one with them.

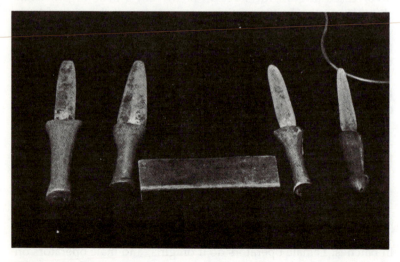

Circumcision knives and sharpening stone (Uganda).

The individual is recognized to be an adult

Initiation is a public recognition that the individual is now passing from childhood to adulthood. The cutting of his flesh is a symbol of getting rid of the period of childhood, and getting ready for the period of adulthood. As long as a person has not gone through initiation, he is regarded as a child. Therefore he is not given full responsibility at home and in the community. Once the initiation has taken place, he is ready to enjoy full privileges and shoulder various responsibilities, both in his immediate family and in the larger community or nation.

Initiation is the gateway to marriage

Initiation gives opportunity to the young people to be prepared for marriage. In fact, one of the features of initiation is the period spent in seclusion, during which they are taught many things concerning the life of their people, its history, its traditions, its beliefs, and above all how to raise a family. The mysteries and secrets of married life are normally revealed to the young people at this point to prepare them for what is soon to come. Nobody is allowed to get married before going through initiation. Therefore initiation is the gateway to marriage; and many people get married soon after it, under normal conditions.

A bridge between youth and adulthood

Initiation is a central bridge in life. It brings together one's youth and adulthood, the period of ignorance and that of knowledge. Separating a person from one stage of life it also joins him to another. The earlier state of seemingly passive life is dramatically brought to an end. The person is officially admitted into the next state which is socially more productive and he or she is authorized to play a full and active part in it, as an integral member of the community. His or her youth gives way or grows into adulthood. It is initiation which also bridges the male with the female, fatherhood with motherhood, since it signals the official permission for one to get married and bear children. It also joins the living with the departed, the visible with the invisible, because after initiation a person may perform religious rituals.

Initiation symbols for male circumcision, showing a dog biting a monkey (Zaire).

Boys during the healing period after circumcision (Tanzania). Their bodies are covered with white chalk, as a symbol of circumcision among their people.

Initiation is a mark of solemn unity and identification. Through it the individual is sealed to his people and his people to him. This is a deeply religious step. For that reason, during the initiation ceremonies and after, the leaders in charge offer sacrifices or prayers to God and ask for his blessings upon the young people. In other places, the spirits are believed or invited to be present to witness the occasion. From that occasion onwards, the initiated boys and girls will forever bear the scars of what is cut on their organs, and these will be scars of identity. Through the scars, the initiated are henceforth identified as members of such and such a people. Without that identification scar, they cannot be fully integrated with their people.

A young man undergoing circumcision, Ovimbundu (Angola).

Education in tribal matters

During the seclusion part of the initiation rites, the young people undergo a period of education or traditional schooling. As we have said, this concerns tribal life and matters which equip them to live now as full members of their society. They also undergo physical training to overcome difficulties and pain, and to cultivate courage, endurance, perseverance and obedience. This educational experience equips them mentally, bodily, emotionally and morally, for adolescence and adulthood. They come away as young adults in the eyes of society.

Returning home is like a new birth

Upon completion of their seclusion, the young people return to their homes. This is often a great occasion of rejoicing and feasting in the community. Returning home is like being born afresh into a new life. They go home as new people, full people, responsible people. In fact, in many parts of Africa, they are given new names following their initiation, to show the radical change they have undergone. They may also wear new clothes, and receive presents from relatives and neighbours. They receive respect from everyone. A new rhythm of life begins for them, and they start to play a new role.

Initiation brings the people together

Initiation is thus an important stage, through which young people in many parts of Africa have to go. It shuts the door to childhood, and opens another one to adulthood. It makes the young people active members of their society, and no longer simply passive children. The spirit of the community is renewed through this periodic initiation with all the feasting that goes with it. The entire people are brought together: the departed, the living and those yet to be born, because now the gate for marriage and family life is opened for the initiates.

• Different Forms of Initiation

Even where circumcision is not practised, there are other ways of marking the transition from childhood to adulthood. This may be done on a family basis, or by the community at large. It may, for example, involve brewing some beer and slaughtering a goat for the older men, who then ceremoniously welcome the young adolescents to their status.

Age sets

In some parts of Africa, such as Kenya, Tanzania, Sierra Leone and others, those who are initiated in the same batch form age sets or societies. They consider themselves to be one. They share what belongs to them, as if they were real brothers or sisters. In the case of the secret societies, they even have their own language and other ways of communicating with one another. These initiation ties are life-long, and they are regarded as very binding.

Changes in traditional customs

We should take note that many of the traditional African customs and ideas concerning birth and the time of youth have been severely disrupted by the Western ways of life which have been introduced to Africa. Fortunately these traditional customs have not died out completely, and in some parts of Africa they are still observed, while in others they are being revived. We cannot go back completely to all the details of traditional life, and while lamenting the loss of some of them, we should also look to the present and the future. Customs connected with birth and the naming of children can with slight modifications continue to be followed; but those concerned with initiation seem difficult to retain as a whole in practice, particularly because of the coming of Western types of schooling. In this the loss is great, but there are also gains in exchange. Whether one is better than the other is a matter of opinion, and it is not the intention of this book to deal with that question.

Having seen young people through the important experience of initiation, which, among other things, prepares them for marriage and family life, let us now move on to that next phase.

10 · Marriage and Family Life

• The Obligation to Get Married

Initiation ceremonies for the young people prepare them for the most responsible phase of their life. This is marriage and the raising of families. Where circumcision and clitoridectomy are practised, they symbolically represent the flow of life through the shedding of blood from the organs of reproduction. This is a profound religious act by means of which the young people accept that they have to become bearers of children, and their communities give approval to that step. Once they have gone through initiation ceremonies, not only is there nothing to stop them from getting married and bearing children, but they are under a solemn obligation to do so.

It is believed in many African societies that from the very beginning of human life, God commanded or taught people to get married and bear children. Therefore marriage is looked upon as a sacred duty which every normal person must perform. Failure to do so means in effect stopping the flow of life through the individual, and hence the diminishing of mankind upon the earth. Anything that deliberately goes towards the destruction or obstruction of human life is regarded as wicked and evil. Therefore anybody who, under normal conditions, refuses to get married, is committing a major offence in the eyes of society and people will be against him. In all African societies everything possible is done to prepare people for marriage and to make them think in terms of marriage.

Myths of the creation of man agree that human life started with husband and wife. It must also continue in the same way. Marriage is the meeting-point for the three layers of human life according to African Religion. These are the departed, the living and those to be born. The departed come into the picture because they are the roots on whom the living stand. The living are the link between death and life. Those to be born are the buds in the loins of the living, and marriage makes it possible for them to germinate and sprout. If one deliberately refuses to get married it means, therefore, that one is cutting off the vital link between death and life, and destroying the buds which otherwise would sprout and grow on the human tree of life.

A daughter receives parental blessings from her mother and father, in preparation for marriage (Nigeria).

We saw that at the beginning, men were given the gift either of immortality, of resurrection or of the ability to become young again. These gifts were all lost for one reason and another, and death came to dwell among people for ever. African Religion does not tell people how to conquer or escape death. What it does emphasize, however, is that through marriage the effects of death are reduced and neutralized considerably. Therefore marriage and childbearing are the medicines against death. While death continues to demolish life, marriage and childbearing keep ahead of it all the time. This makes sure that even if individuals die, human life as such does not die. Death captures individuals along the road, but because of marriage and childbearing it cannot keep pace with human life at large.

The obligation to get married is, therefore, the only means of human survival as far as the views of African peoples are concerned. For that reason it is a religious obligation. It is as old as human society. Through marriage and childbearing, human life is preserved, propagated and perpetuated. Through them life is also deepened vertically and spread out horizontally. Therefore marriage and childbearing are the focus of life. They are at the very centre of human existence, just as man is at the very centre of the universe.

• Marriage Customs

Since marriage is at the centre of human life, it is to be expected that there should be many marriage customs, throughout Africa. It is not the purpose of this book to describe these customs, which include methods of choosing the marriage partner, engagements, weddings, husband-and-wife relationships, the setting up of a family, relationships between the couple and other relatives, rules governing whom not to marry, separation, divorce, inheritance,

This woman is wearing a long chain on her right ear as a symbol of marriage and motherhood (Tanzania).

and many other aspects. There are many books which describe all or some of these aspects, one of which is *Love and Marriage in Africa* by J. S. Mbiti. Our purpose here is simply to look briefly at the religious meaning of marriage and family life. Therefore we cannot discuss all the various aspects of marriage, which is a complex institution.

Choosing marriage partners

In some parts of Africa, parents choose marriage partners for their children even before they are born. This is to make absolutely sure that they do get someone to marry. In other parts the choice is made for the young people by their relatives. Another custom is to let the young people themselves find the person they wish to marry, and then inform their parents or other relatives. The opportunities for them to do this are provided by social gatherings, dances and communal work, and by their knowing other people in the neighbourhood.

There are in all African societies, regulations concerning those that one may not marry. These are most often people of one's own clan, and relatives of one's mother or father up to a certain degree of kinship. In every African society people know how they are related to others through blood kinship and marriage relationships. Therefore people know who is a close relative and whom they cannot marry. The clan system helps in many parts of Africa, because often a person is not allowed to marry someone of the same clan. It is believed that marriage to a forbidden person will result in misfortune, perhaps in the death of the couple or more often of their children. The community will, in most cases, refuse to sanction such marriages, and anyone who disobeys cuts himself off from his social group and may be regarded as the cause of any misfortunes which befall his relatives and community.

Whatever method is followed in choosing the marriage partner, the families and relatives of the two sides must be involved before the marriage can take place. In some places it is the custom to have a go-between who will negotiate between the two families concerned. In other places it is the parents of the groom who approach those of the girl, and establish an engagement relationship. All over Africa, the custom is observed of exchanging visits and gifts among the members of the two families and their relatives. This eventually leads to arrangements for exchanging marriage gifts which the parents of the girl ask from those of the boy.

Marriage gifts

The point about the marriage gifts is that they are the outward symbols of a serious undertaking by the families concerned. They bind the man and the wife together in the sight of their families. They are the symbols of the marriage bond or covenant. They seal up the sacred relationship established through marriage, a relationship which will be worked out over a long period of time. Marriage gifts are the legal instruments which authorize the husband and wife to live together and to bear children, and which constantly remind them that they must continue to live together. If the marriage eventually breaks down, many of these gifts are normally returned, as a sign of failure. The gifts may consist of foodstuffs, drinks, money, cattle, sheep, goats, utensils, ornaments, tools and other material things, and possibly also of work done by the groom and his relatives for those of the bride. The gifts are given during engagement and continued after marriage. They are not to be regarded as payment for the wife, even if some greedy parents today act as though they were selling their daughters to get money. It is truer to say that these gifts show how much the husband appreciates the care that the wife's parents have taken over her. She is not to be taken for granted, and the fact that her husband gives gifts to her parents, for her sake, adds to her dignity as a partner.

Marriage establishes relationships between families

In traditional African marriage customs, the relatives of the husband and of the wife establish a close relationship through the interchange of visits and gifts. This is an important African view of marriage, namely that it is not an affair between two people only but between those two people together with their families and relatives. This has grown out of the African view that a person does not exist all by himself: he exists because of the existence of other people. The philosophical formula about this says, 'I am because we are, and since we are therefore I am'.

Marriage in the traditional African view is an affair of more than two people. Therefore through marriage many relationships are established, and the married couple are very much in the public eye. For this reason, weddings are carried out with celebrations and festivals, giving an opportunity for everyone to be involved.

Wedding ceremonies vary from people to people. We cannot deal with them here, except to mention some of the ideas lying behind them. In some parts of Africa it is the custom for the groom to go with his friends and stage a mock attack on the people of the bride, so that they capture her and take her away to become his wife. This custom not only provides a lot of fun but adds drama to the event. In other places, when the date for the wedding is arranged the groom's people go to those of the bride and receive her ceremoniously or even without any formal ceremony. In some places it is an accepted form of wedding for the man to run away with the engaged girl, as if they were eloping. When this happens, the parents of the man wake up one morning and find their daughter-in-law already there in the house. Then they formalize the marriage in whatever way custom demands.

Generally feasting and celebration follow the wedding ceremony. In many areas this lasts several days, during which time relatives pay their visits to the couple and other formalities are fulfilled. It is the custom in some areas for the wife, or both wife and husband, to be secluded for several days after the initial wedding. The seclusion in a house, followed by exposure to the public afterwards, is a symbolic way of showing that the couple are being born into a new life, that they are coming out of the womb (of the house). Their 'birth' into married status is greeted with jubilation, and people join in wishing them well.

Rituals and ceremonies accompany or follow the occasion of the wedding. The aim of these is to pray for the welfare of the new couple, to bless them so that they will bear children and to give them instructions and rules on how to conduct themselves as married people. At these rituals, God and the living dead of the family may be called upon to witness the occasion and to give their blessings to the new husband and wife. In many places the bride and her husband are dressed up for these ceremonies and rituals to symbolize the new phase of life into which they now enter. One of the highly valued moments is when the relatives and neighbours find out whether or not the girl was virgin up to the moment of marriage. This is taken so seriously in some societies that should the girl be found to have lost her virginity before marriage, the whole marriage is dissolved there and then, to the shame of the girl's relatives. In the past such a girl might even be killed. If a girl is found to be still a virgin, there is great rejoicing. She and her family are praised and respected by everybody, and often they are given presents. The point here is that one should not play about with those parts of the body through which procreation takes place until and unless the right arrangements have been made for marriage to take place and be consummated. Obviously the question of virginity is not treated in the same way in all African societies, and there are some in which sexual activities are permitted before marriage. Unfortunately no male 'virginity' is tested and, in my opinion, it is unfair to expect girls alone to be tested.

• The Meaning of Marriage in African Societies

According to the way African peoples look at marriage, it has several meanings and purposes. We can mention these now.

The obligation to bear children

Marriage fulfils the obligation, the duty and the custom that every normal person should get married and bear children. This is believed to go back to the very beginning of human life. Failure to get married is like committing a crime against traditional beliefs and practices.

A uniting link in the rhythm of life

Marriage is the uniting link in the rhythm of life. All generations are bound together in the act of marriage – past, present and future generations. The past generations are many but they are represented in one's parents; the present generation is represented in one's own life, and future generations begin to come on the stage through childbearing.

The building of a family

The supreme purpose of marriage according to African peoples is to bear children, to build a family, to extend life, and to hand down the living torch of human existence. For that reason, a marriage becomes fully so only when one or more children have been born. It is a very tragic thing when no children come out of a marriage. Then people do not consider it to be truly a marriage, and other arrangements are made to obtain children in the family.

New relationships between families

Marriage provides for new social relationships to be established between the families and relatives involved. It extends the web of kinship socially.

Remembrance of parents after death

Through marriage and childbearing, the parents are remembered by their children when they die. Anyone who dies without leaving behind a child or close relative to remember him or pour out libations for him is a very unfortunate person. Therefore marriage is intimately linked up with the religious beliefs about the continuation of life beyond death.

Regaining a lost immortality

Marriage is also regarded as the counter-measure against the lost immortality which is talked about in so many traditional myths. Through marriage the departed are in effect 'reborn', not in their total being but by having some of their physical features and characteristics or personality traits reborn in the children of the family. If no children were born these traits and features of the departed members of the family would not be seen again.

Bringing people together

While death takes away individuals one by one and disperses families, the purpose of marriage is to bring people together, to increase them, to multiply them, to keep them alive.

Giving a status in society

Marriage puts the individual and his family on the social, religious and physical map of his community. Everyone recognizes that the individual is a full person when he or she is married and has children. The life of the individual is extended beyond death by the fact of being married and bearing children, because these children survive him and remain a constant evidence that their father and mother once existed. The son or daughter subsequently keeps up the memory of the parents. The more children a person has, the higher is his status in society.

Giving a person 'completeness'

Marriage is the one experience without which a person is not considered to be complete, 'perfect', and truly a man or a woman. It makes a person really 'somebody'. It is part of the definition of who a person is according to African views about man. Without marriage a person is only a human being minus.

Creation of good personal qualities

A happy married and family life creates other aspects of marriage such as love, good character, hard work, beauty, companionship, caring for one another, parental responsibility towards children and the children's responsibility towards their parents. These are qualities which grow in marriage, in the African setting. It is as if people would say, 'Get married first, and these other things will follow if you make a success of your marriage'. Such a philosophy has its risks, but African peoples seem to take these risks and make their marriages work.

Multiple marriages

Because of these views of the meaning and purpose of marriage, additional customs are found in African societies such as marrying several wives, inheriting the wife of a deceased brother (or husband of a deceased sister), arranging for a dead son to be married in absence, arranging for the wives of impotent or long-absent husbands to have children by close relatives or friends, and so on. Where these customs are followed, they are respected and accepted without any feelings of wrongness about them. They are meant to ensure that nobody is left out of marriage, and that children are produced for each family concerned. These customs work in their own way within the traditional setting of African life. Modern changes are making it harder and harder for them all to be followed today, but they have not been altogether abandoned.

• Children and Family Life

We have seen that according to the African views of marriage, its main purpose is to produce children. Children are greatly valued in African life. They are the seal of marriage. In many parts of the continent, once a marriage has produced children, it is very rare to see it broken up, since nobody wishes to part with his or her

A mother carrying her baby on her back (Nigeria). This is a common traditional method of carrying babies, and they seem to enjoy it!

children. On the other hand, if no children are born that marriage often breaks up, although arrangements may be made to preserve it but to get children at the same time. If the wife is barren, then she and her husband may arrange for him to have another wife so that children can be born in that family. If the problem lies with the husband, then a close relative or friend is asked or allowed to sleep with the wife in order that she may bear children for the family.

Children prolong the life of their parents, and through them the name of the family is perpetuated. Therefore children are the glory of the marriage, and the more a person has the bigger is his glory. That is the traditional view, but of course the economic conditions of modern life are beginning to undermine this view.

A high value is put upon bearing children who, among other things, will later on look after their ageing parents. This photograph shows an old man with his son and grandson caring for him in his extreme age (Kenya).

114

Children add to the social stature of the family, and both girls and boys have their social usefulness in the eyes of their families. Where inheritance is through the father, it is very important to have sons so that the family line of inheritance may be maintained. They become the heirs, and African people do not wish to die without heirs. Where inheritance is through the mother, the same case will apply to having daughters.

At home there are duties which the children are expected to do as their share in the life of the family. They are taught obedience and respect towards their parents and other older people. They help in the work around the house and in the fields, in looking after cattle, fishing and hunting, building houses, going on errands, learning the trade or skills of their parent, and in many other ways. As they grow older they gradually acquire a different social status and their responsibilities increase, so that they take a greater share in the life of the family. When the parents become old and weak it is the duty of the children, especially the heirs or sons, to look after the parents and the affairs of the family. Finally when the parents die it is the duty of their surviving children to bury them properly, to remember them, to look after their graves, to give bits of food and pour libations to them where this is the custom, and to keep a good relationship with their departed parents who are now spirits of the living dead.

Thus, the children are introduced gradually to the physical, economic, social and religious lives of their families. Without them the concept of the family would grind to a halt. For African peoples the family includes children, parents, grandparents, and other relatives such as brothers, sisters, cousins and so on. All relatives have duties and responsibilities towards one another. Everyone knows how he is related to other people in the clan and the neighbourhood. The idea of the family also extends to include the departed, as well as those who are about to be born. This family concept spreads vertically and horizontally. The individual does not just exist alone: he exists because others exist. He must, therefore, play his full role in that interdependence of existence.

In African life, we cannot speak of marriage alone. It is always in terms of marriage and family life. One gets married within the context of family life, and one gets married in order to enlarge that family life. One stands on the roots of family life; and one puts out branches of family life. This idea of the individual in relation to marriage and family life is deeply rooted in African thinking.

11 · Death and the Hereafter

• The Origin of Death

There are hundreds and hundreds of myths all over Africa concerning ideas about the origin of death. Some of them have been collected in books (like those listed in Appendix B). Many myths, though, remain uncollected and unrecorded. Death is one of the most universal and mysterious experiences. It is not surprising, therefore, that there are so many myths about its origin, and so many ideas seeking to explain it. In this chapter we shall look at some of these ideas.

We said in Chapter 8 that originally man was intended to live forever. For that reason God gave the first men one or more of the three gifts of immortality, resurrection and the ability to become young again. But all these three were lost and death came into the world. There are different explanations as to how the loss took place and how death came about.

In many myths spreading all over eastern, central and southern Africa, it is said that God sent a message to the first men that they would either live for ever or rise again if they died. This message was given to one of the animals to take to men. The animal is often said to have been the chameleon. But the chameleon lingered on the way and delayed the message. Meanwhile God sent another but faster animal, usually said to have been a bird, lizard or hare, with another message that people would die. The latter message reached people before that of immortality or resurrection, and since then death has remained in the world.

There are other versions of this myth. For example in Sierra Leone it is said that God sent at the same time a dog with a message of immortality and a toad with a message of death. On the way the dog stopped to eat. So the toad reached men first and delivered its message. The dog, with a full stomach, arrived too late.

In several myths scattered all over Africa, it is said that God forbade the first people to eat either a certain fruit, or eggs, or animals. When they ate this forbidden food, death came to them.

In Rwanda and Burundi the story goes that God used to hunt death if it appeared. He told people to remain indoors and not to give shelter to death if they saw it running away. One woman, however, went to work in her field, and while she was there death came and asked for protection. She allowed it to hide under her clothes or, in another version, to get into her mouth. God came with his hunting dogs chasing after it, and when in his great wisdom he found that the woman had hidden it, he told her and the people to keep death thereafter.

There are other stories which say that God gave people a bundle or vessel with a secret in it, and forbade them to open it. Overcome by curiosity, or through a mistake, someone opened this vessel or bag, and out came death.

These and many more myths emphasize that death came almost by mistake, and that since then it has remained among men. The blame is laid upon people themselves, animals and in some cases spirits or monsters. Even though all these myths speak about how death came about, there are no myths in Africa about how death might one day be overcome or removed from the world. Thus, death spoilt the original paradise of men, according to African beliefs. Death also meant a separation of God from men, and the coming of many sorrows and agonies upon men.

In addition to the myths about the origin of death, people try to visualize death in personal terms. Some think of it as a monster, others as an animal, and many regard it as a kind of spirit. It is said in Uganda, for example, that the spirit of death never laughs. And who cam blame it, since its work is to kill, destroy, take away, and terrorize people everywhere.

• How Death is Caused in Human Life

Even though people believe that death came into the world at a very early date in the history of mankind, they believe also that every time a person dies this death is 'caused'. There are several ways in which it is caused.

Death by sorcery

People believe that sorcery, witchcraft and evil magic cause death. Therefore, when someone has died, people often try to find out who used sorcery, witchcraft or magic against the dead person. Someone is often blamed for it, and in some cases the suspect may be beaten to death, fined or thrown out of the district. Relatives of the deceased may also take other types of revenge which are less open.

Death caused by spirits

If the blame is not laid on the use of sorcery, witchcraft or evil magic against the dead person, spirits may be blamed. These might be spirits of people who have had a grudge against the person, or whose bodies were not properly buried, or who have been neglected by their relatives for some reason or another. Deaths caused by spirits are rare, since in most cases people always find or suspect someone in the village to be the cause.

Death by a curse

Curses, broken taboos or oaths are sometimes believed to cause deaths. Therefore they are feared, and people endeavour to avoid being cursed or breaking oaths.

Natural death

It is sometimes believed that God may call old people to leave this life. This is, however, rare, and only in a few societies is such a belief entertained. The first three are the main causes of death, and God is normally left out of the picture, even though people believe that if he did not allow it the person would not die.

There are always physical causes and circumstances surrounding every death. These include sickness, disease, old age, accident, lightning, earthquake, flood, drowning, animal attack, and many others. But African peoples believe that a particular person will only die from one of these physical causes because some human or other agent has brought it about by means of a curse, witchcraft, magic and so on. These are what we may call the mystical causes of death. People often wish to know both the physical and mystical causes of death; it is not enough for them to find out only the physical causes. They take much trouble to establish the mystical causes as well, and this is done through consulting diviners and medicine men, or by suspicion and guesswork.

• The Act of Dying

Many words are used all over Africa concerning the actual act of dying. We need to mention only some of these as examples. People refer to dying as returning home, going away, answering the summons, saying 'yes' to death, disappearing, departing, ceasing to eat, ceasing to breathe, sinking, fighting a losing battle, refusing food, rejecting people, sleeping, taking one way, saying goodbye, shutting the eyes, being broken up, being snatched away, being taken away, being called away, joining the forefathers, becoming God's property, and so on.

All these words show the belief that death is not a complete destruction of the individual. Life goes on beyond the grave. Therefore people combine their sorrow over the death of someone with the belief that that is not the end and that the departed continues to live in the hereafter. We shall consider this point further in another section below.

• Rituals of Death

Death is sorrowful. It is also important. There are, therefore, many complex and even long rituals and ceremonies associated with death. In every African society people are very sensitive to what is done when there is a death in the family. Death marks a physical separation of the individual from other human beings. This is a radical change, and the funeral rites and ceremonies are intended to draw attention to that permanent separation. Meticulous care is taken to fulfil the funeral rites, and to avoid causing any offence to the departed. This is not done for unknown strangers, for thieves, murderers, witches and other trouble-makers in the community, or for those who have died abnormal deaths.

Disposal of the body

There are rituals concerning the preparation of the corpse for disposal. In some places it is washed either with water or with water and traditional medicines. In other areas it is shaved and the nails are cut off. There are places where oil or butter is put through the mouth and nostrils, ears and other bodily openings. Skins, leather, cotton, clothes, bark clothes, or leaves are used to cover the corpse, and the whole body is in some places anointed with ghee or other oil. For all these preparations, there are ritual leaders and elders in every village. Some individuals are not allowed to touch or come near to the corpse in case misfortune should befall them or the family. These are usually the children, pregnant women, or suspected witches. The preparation for burial may be done ritually or without formality.

Generally the disposal of the body takes place the same or the following day. This is mainly because of the tropical heat which makes the body decompose fast. However, nowadays in some areas the corpse is kept frozen in the hospital or mortuary for several days, while funeral preparations are being made and relatives living far away are awaited. In most parts of Africa burial is the usual means of disposing of the body of a dead person. It may take place in the backyard of one of the houses in the village, in a family burial place, or at the original place of birth. The grave may be rectangular, oval, cave-like, or even a big pot made for that purpose.

Formerly other methods of disposal were used in some places, such as throwing the body in the bush to be eaten by animals and birds, throwing it into a running stream or river, or keeping it in a small house nearby so that it would decompose completely until the bare skeleton was left. This would then be buried or otherwise kept.

Burial of belongings with the body

It is the custom in many parts of Africa to bury some belongings with the body, such as spears, bows and arrows, stools, snuff, foodstuffs, beads, ornaments, money, tools and domestic utensils. Some of these things might be placed on the grave afterwards. Formerly in some places servants and wives of kings or other rich people were also buried with the body. The belief behind this custom is that the departed needs weapons to defend himself along the way to the next world, or food to eat on the journey, wives and servants to keep him company when he reaches there, and other property to use so that he would not arrive empty-handed or remain poor. The greatest treasures ever discovered in a burial place were those of King Tutankhamen of Egypt who died in B.C. 1352. These were discovered in his tomb in upper Egypt nearly 3,300 years later, in 1922. They comprised jewels, furniture, shrines and portrait masks all covered with gold, worth an inestimable amount of money. Many other treasures and valuables have been buried with people all over Africa. Most perish within a short time but others may survive the process of rotting, weathering and rusting for many years. Precisely why the supposed owners do not remove and take them away with them to that other world, we may never know. But they do not seem to mind if someone among the living helps himself to their unclaimed treasures or property from their grave.

Funeral rites

The size and importance of a funeral varies according to the person concerned. For children and unmarried people the funeral is usually simple and attended only by close relatives. For a chief or king, it is a national affair which involves the suspension of normal life in order that people may pay their last respects to their dead king or queen. These major funerals require a lot of preparation, they involve a great deal of pomp and a lot of wealth is spent on them. In today's nations, a dead head of state (or president) is given a pompous and costly funeral, attended by other heads of state and diplomatic representatives. For Christians, Muslims or followers of other religions, funeral rites of their respective religions are followed, as the case may be.

In many parts of Africa, part of the funeral ceremony involves the selection and installation of the heir of the family, the chiefdom or the kingdom. This can be a complicated affair where political or economic interests are involved. But in most societies the oldest son, daughter, niece or nephew of the deceased person is the successor and new head of the family or kingdom.

Various rites are performed at the actual burial or other disposal of the body. These rites are intended to send off the departed peacefully, to sever his links with the living, and to ensure that normal life continues among the survivors. People, especially women, wail and weep, lamenting the departure of the dead person, recalling the good things he said and did, and reminding themselves that he lives on in the next world.

Feasting and songs of mourning

Feasting follows the funeral rites. This is partly to comfort the bereaved and to bring life back to normal, and partly to thank those who have officiated in the funeral rites. In some parts of Africa it is the custom for people to fast for a day or two following someone's death, and this fast is broken by the communal feasting afterwards. It is also the custom to stop work for a few days, as a sign of respect for the dead person. In many places members of the immediate family have their hair shaved off, and some of their normal activities are suspended until all the funeral rites have been performed. The shaving of the hair is a symbol of separation, showing that one of the family has been separated from them. At the same time it is an indication of people's belief that death does not destroy life, since the growth of new hair indicates that life continues to spring up.

Various signs and symbols are used to show that death has occurred in the family. The shaving of the hair is one of the commonest. People smear themselves with white clay in some places, as a sign of death and mourning; in others they refrain from washing their bodies and clothes for several days or months; certain bulls or goats may be killed to mark the death of someone. Sometimes animals go without being milked for several days; people suspend sleeping with their marriage partners for several weeks or months; pots are broken up in the houses; certain houses in the homestead are abandoned for good, as an indication that someone has died; and many other things are done.

By doing these things people are able to come to terms with the agonies, sorrows and disruption caused by death. By ritualizing death, people dance it away, drive it away, and renew their own life after it has taken away one of their members.

• The Hereafter

On the question of the hereafter or the next world, African peoples have many ideas. As a whole these ideas paint the hereafter in features, colours and descriptions, which are very much like those of the present life. This is to be expected since, if the hereafter was terribly different from the present life, people would find it disturbing to their imagination and would feel that they would become strangers in that world when they die. This would make them resent death more.

In many parts of Africa, people believe that the next world is invisible but very close to that of the living. We have already come across this idea when we considered African views of the universe. The hereafter is in this view next to this world, and for the majority of people it is situated on the same earth. It has rivers, mountains, lakes, forests, homesteads, fields, cattle, sheep, goats, dogs, chickens, wild animals, and all the things we find in our physical life. But we cannot see them, although the spirits who live there are believed to be able to see what we are doing.

Where the dead live

For some societies, the departed remain in the neighbourhood of their human homestead. They are still part of the family, as we

A conical grave, showing gourds, sticks, spade heads, lamp, etc. for the departed (Sudan).

mentioned elsewhere. Their surviving relatives and friends feel that the departed are close to them, and that people may even walk on them since their graves are close at hand.

In other societies it is held that the land of the departed is in the woods, forests, river banks, or hills somewhere in the country. Such places are, therefore, often avoided, and people may not build homes or cultivate fields there. They do not wish to disturb the departed.

There are other peoples who hold that the land of the departed is situated somewhere underground – the underworld – or that it is beyond some rivers or forests or lakes. For others, it is thought to be in desert or desolate places away from the homesteads. As such, the dead have to travel several hours or days to get there, and it is for this reason that they are buried with food and weapons for use on the way.

In a very few cases it is thought that the world of the departed is somewhere in the sky, or that the spirits of the departed eventually go to live in the sky. They are then associated with the moon and stars, but not with the sun, as this would be too hot for them! In Nigeria some people believe that the dead appear before

God to receive their judgment depending on what they have done with their lives. They are then sent to a good place where they rejoin their relatives who departed before them, or to a bad place where they remain in misery for a long time until eventually God takes pity on them. This idea of some people being punished after death is not common in Africa, and the only other place where it is reported is in a small area of Ghana. We may say, therefore, that on the whole African Religion has neither heaven nor hell, and neither rewards nor punishment for people in the hereafter.

Life continues more or less the same in the hereafter as it did in this world. Funeral rites are aimed at marking the separation of the departed from the living, even though it is believed that the dead continue to live in the hereafter. The gate between these two seems to open only one way, and once a person has died he cannot return to human life in his total being. Let us see what happens to his spirit or soul.

• The Destiny of the Soul

It is held in African societies that a person is made up of body and spirit (or soul, life, breath, shadow or double). There are other parts, but these two are the main ones. They have to be joined together to make a living person. It is not known exactly when the soul joins the body. Among some people it is believed that this takes place when the husband and wife sleep together at the conception of the child-to-be. In others it is thought that the soul joins the body some time before birth, or shortly after birth. There are even places where it is believed that a person has two souls or spirits, one of which may wander about when he is asleep.

The spirit leaves the body

Death is recognized as the point when the spirit separates from the body. Because the spirit is closely associated with breathing, people know that the spirit has gone when a person stops breathing. Some think that it goes out through the mouth or nostrils or eyes.

Even though the spirit leaves the body, it is thought in many parts of Africa that for a while it lingers on around the body or homestead. For that reason, the right funeral rites must be performed to send it off, to enable it to go away, and to let it join other spirits. People imagine that even if the body remains behind, the spirit is still distinguishable by more or less the same features as it had when the person lived. This does not mean that the spirit puts on another body. African ideas are not clear on this point. But at least the spirit does not lose the identity it had when it was a living person.

The living dead

While surviving relatives remember the departed, the spirit more or less leads a personal continuation of life. It has become what we have called the living dead. People regard it as being much like a human being although it is dead. If it appears to members of the family, they will say that they saw 'So and so'. Up to that point it has not lost its personal name and identity. During this period which may last up to four or even five generations, it is possible for something of the features, characteristics and personality of

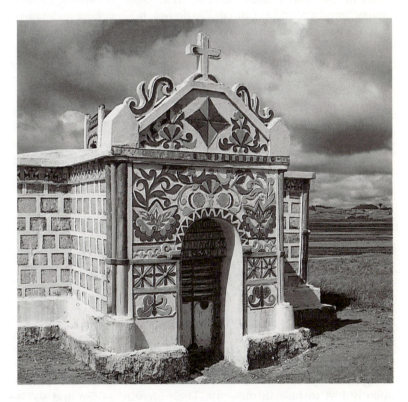

Merina tomb, decorated in memory of a dead relative (Madagascar).

such a spirit (the living dead) to be noticed in a newly born child. Then people would say that 'So and so' has come back, has returned, or has been reborn. The child may then be given the name of that deceased person, or people may make sacrifices and offerings to express joy and gratitude. This idea of partial rebirth is spoken of as reincarnation. But not everyone is reborn in that manner, nor is the entire deceased person reborn as such. Only some aspects of the living dead are reborn, and this is perfectly possible biologically. Furthermore, those aspects can be inherited by either boys or girls regardless of the sex of the living dead in question. They can also be reproduced simultaneously in several children within the family.

Other manifestations of the living dead are said to occur in dreams, visions, possessions and certain illnesses or mental disturbances. In dreams and visions, people claim to encounter the spirit of the living dead, to talk to it, and to receive certain instructions or requests from it. We do not, however, have detailed descriptions of what these living dead really look like, other than being told by those who see them that they saw 'So and so'. Presumably they appear more or less the way they did before they died.

In spirit possessions and illnesses, the help of the diviner or medicine man is often necessary in order to find out which spirit of the living dead it is and what it may want. If a living dead makes demands which can be fulfilled, people normally meet them. But if the demands are impossible, other ways of keeping the living dead quiet are sought through the medicine man or diviner. Sometimes the spirits of those who died away from their homes, or those who were not properly buried, may demand ritual transfer to their home compound or reburial of their remains. For this reason, even in modern life, Africans who die in the cities and towns are often taken to their original homesteads for burial. Sometimes these burial rites are performed according to Christian or Muslim services, as well as in African traditional ways.

Ghosts

After four or five generations, the living dead are finally forgotten personally because those who knew them while they were human beings will by then have died as well. Their spirits are consequently lost to human memory. Their identity as 'So and so' is forever eclipsed as far as people are concerned, unless the spirit

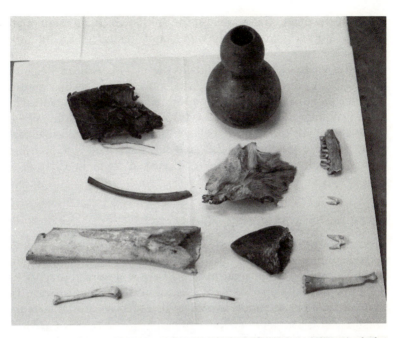

The gourd is used to store beer for family spirits; the bones and teeth symbolise animals that have been sacrificed; the hoof is for contacting the spirits in the morning and evening (Uganda).

possesses someone and gives a full identity of itself. Although the spirit is still a human spirit, it is no longer a living dead, it becomes the ghost of an unknown person. It has no personal interest in any human family. Nobody remembers it at meal-times or during offerings and sacrifices. It really withdraws from human activities and becomes fully a member of the spirit beings. It may wander about, but nobody knows it. It may enter and stay in trees, lakes, rivers, rocks, animals, and so on. Or it may just disappear to congregate with other spirits in the world of spirits. Such are the spirits which people fear if they meet them, because they are strangers and people do not know how to act in front of strange spirits. Sometimes these spirits attack people through an outbreak of possession or an epidemic, and then the people drive them away with ceremonies. Some of these unknown spirits may be used by witches and other individuals who wish to do harm to their neighbours. Others are used in divination and medical practices to help in the diagnosis of diseases and problems and their cure or solution. Some mediums and diviners call back the spirits of the dead. These are also the spirits which are mentioned in folk stories, often exaggerated and distorted for literary purposes.

Exactly whether the spirits finally die or not, African Religion does not say. Since they are spirits, nobody can really be sure whether they only disappear from human memory or whether in some way their numbers decrease through a kind of death. All we know is that African peoples believe that there is an invisible part of the universe and that this part is thickly populated with invisible beings including the spirits. We discussed them in Chapter 7 above.

• Remembering the Departed

African peoples believe that death is not the end of human life. A person continues to exist in the hereafter. This continuation of life beyond death is recognized through a very widespread practice of remembering the departed, which is found throughout Africa. In some areas more attention is paid to it, especially in the farming

A family shrine and altar where sacrifices are frequently made (Nigeria).

A skull kept in a broken pot, in memory of a dead relative (Tanzania).

communities, than is customary in nomadic and pastoral communities.

This remembrance of the dead concerns mainly the living dead, that is, the spirits of those who died up to four or five generations back. Heads of families, adults and married people are remembered in this way longer than babies, children and the unmarried.

Food and drink for the dead

In many parts of Africa, adult members of the family, and especially the heads of families, pour out beer, water, milk or some other beverage on the ground for the spirits of the family. They may also put bits of food on the ground for the same purpose. In many countries, such as Sierra Leone, Ghana, Nigeria, Uganda and elsewhere, there are often family shrines in the homestead or behind the houses, set apart for remembering the departed. Here kola nuts, coffee beans, blood, beer and other food items are placed, with words to the effect that the food is being given to those who have departed (sometimes mentioning their names). In some areas the placing of foodstuffs is done daily, in others only occasionally.

Consultation and ritual

Another method of remembering the departed is to consult them through the diviner, medicine man or medium, when a major family undertaking or decision is about to be made, or when there is a major illness.

During family ceremonies and rituals, such as those that mark the birth and initiation of children, the departed are often remembered in a definite way.

Naming the dead in prayers

It is the custom in some parts of Africa to mention the names of departed relatives when one is praying to God. These departed members of the family are believed to relay the prayers to God, since it is considered rude in those societies to approach God directly unless it is absolutely necessary.

Naming children after the dead

The departed are also remembered by naming children after them, especially if their features have been inherited by those children. In some places, animals such as bulls or goats may be dedicated to the departed, and slaughtered for them or in their honour when it is thought they may need them.

Thus in African life, the departed are not readily forgotten, though there may be taboos against mentioning their names in certain places. Through rituals, dreams, visions, possessions and names they are recalled and respected. This does not and cannot mean that they are worshipped. The departed are considered to be still alive, and people show by these practices that they recognise their presence. In this way, African Religion is being realistic, since nobody wants to be forgotten by his family immediately after dying.

12 • Rituals and Festivals

• **The Meaning and Importance of Rituals**

A rite or ritual is a set form of carrying out a religious action or ceremony. It is a means of communicating something of religious significance, through word, symbol and action. Therefore a ritual embodies a belief or beliefs. The ritual word is powerful since it is spoken in seriousness and solemnity, and it is repeated every time that ritual is done.

There are innumerable rituals and ceremonies in African Religion. At the beginning of this book we said that there are no sacred books in African Religion. Instead, it is a living religion which is written in the lives of the people. Africans celebrate life. Therefore they celebrate their religion, they dance it, they sing it, they act it. A lot of the visible demonstration of African Religion occurs in rituals and festivals. These embody what people believe, what they value, and what they wish to apply in daily life. Through rituals, people not only act their religion but communicate it to the younger generation.

Different kinds of ritual

There is a wide variety of rituals in African Religion. Some concern the life of the individual from before birth to after death. We have already considered many of these. Others are specifically for the wider community, embracing its total life and activities. These cover the rhythm of the year with its seasons and the activities that people carry out. There are other rituals which are performed occasionally, as when there is a war, raids, a locust invasion or a natural calamity. Rituals generate a sense of certainty and familiarity. They provide continuity and unity among those who perform or attend them. In turn people find a degree of identity through this common observance and experience. For example, the young people who go through the same rite of circumcision are bound together into a unity, and each finds his own identity within the unity of that group.

Through the ritual action and word, people feel able to exercise a certain amount of control over the invisible world and the forces of nature. In this way man feels himself to be not just a passive creature in the universe, but a creative agent. For the purposes of ritual he uses almost everything at his disposal, including symbols and colours, incantations, oral formulas – especially invocations and prayers – and the help of mystical powers if necessary.

Because there are so many rituals in African Religion, we shall not be able to describe them one by one. Instead, we shall now look at the different types of rituals and see what role they play in the life of the individual and the community.

• Personal Rituals

We have already come across most of these. They are the rituals performed along the life's journey of the individual. They begin during pregnancy. They continue at birth, naming, teething, during puberty, at circumcision or clitoridectomy, in other forms of initiation, at engagement, marriage, childbearing, eldership, old age, death and when one has become a living dead. Thus, the life of the individual is accompanied by rituals. In addition to personal rituals, he also takes part in communal rituals and the rituals of other individuals. Obviously rituals are not observed at each and every one of these stages listed above in each African society. For some peoples only birth, initiation, marriage and burial are considered sufficiently important to be marked by rituals and ceremonies. In other societies naming, title-giving, and eldership may be the most important.

Personal rituals draw attention to the uniqueness of the individual. They tell him and the world around that he matters, that he is valuable, and that he is a member of the wider community. They also separate him from one status and introduce him to another. For example, the initiation rites terminate a person's status as a child, and confer on him the status of adulthood. They separate him from one phase but link him up to another. The new status brings new responsibilities and rights, and these are ritually handed over to him. Therefore, psychologically the ritual concerned gives the individual confidence in himself, and stimulates him to conduct himself with courage in his new status.

Pregnancy rituals are for the purpose of blessing and protecting the mother and foetus (unborn baby). Birth rituals announce or recognise the arrival of the child and its separation from the mother, and provide an opportunity to bless her and the baby. At death the rituals send off the departed and normalize life for the survivors. In these three cases of personal rituals, the individual

Masks of the Gelede society, 'to placate the mothers' and to show the procreational power of mothers (Nigeria).

concerned is passive, since he cannot participate actively. Other people act on his behalf. In the other types of personal rituals, he is often an active participant and knows what is going on.

Festivals accompany all the major rituals of personal life. They are occasions that bring people together to form a corporate group. Their oneness is renewed as they eat together, rejoice together and often dance together.

• Agricultural Rituals

African peoples have through the centuries lived by farming, stock-keeping, hunting and fishing, as well as by food-gathering in some cases. Many rituals have been evolved to cover all these means of livelihood, incorporating what people believe, the values they attach to those activities and the right procedures or behaviour required to make them run smoothly. Let us look at the agricultural rituals first, which may be divided into two groups.

Farming rituals

These are the rituals that have to do with the earth, the soil, the crops and the seasons. There are many of them among every African people. The commonest and most important of all is the rain-making ritual. In many countries of Africa there are specialists who look after this ritual. They are well trained in matters of the weather. In some places their office is hereditary; and they may have additional responsibilities like the famous rain-making queen of the Lovedu in southern Africa. Rain-making ceremonies are at the heart of the people's welfare since much of the life in African countries depends on rain.

The term 'rain-making' is perhaps a wrong name for this ritual. The ceremony is chiefly an occasion for praying for rain. Rain-makers do not produce rain as such. They perform rituals including sacrifices and offerings, in order to pray publicly for rain especially when the rainy season seems to be delayed. Rain-makers know their weather secrets well, and time their rituals carefully to coincide with the period when the rains should be starting. There are also rituals performed to reduce or stop rain if too much is falling.

The seasonal coming of the rains renews the activities of the community, as well as reviving the life of plants and insects and animals. Therefore the rain-making ritual, which often comes before the start of the rains, is a religious act of renewing life, sanctifying life, reviving life, for both human beings and other creatures. Through this ritual man is playing the role of the priest of nature around him.

Rituals in making new fields

There are rituals performed when people clear forests or bushes for a new field. The rituals serve as a way of removing danger and blessing the use of the new fields. We have seen that people believe that there are innumerable spirits, some of which occupy trees and forests. Where that belief exists, it is thought necessary to perform rituals which, among other things, will send away these spirits from the bushes and trees being cleared away to make a new field. If such a ritual is not done, it is feared that the people who work on that field may be molested by the spirits or may meet with mysterious misfortunes. The ritual removes such fear and danger, and helps the people to find harmony with their new field.

Planting rituals

There are rituals for planting seeds, for weeding, for tasting the first fruits, for harvesting and even for putting the food in store. The aim of these rituals is mainly to bless people's work in the fields, to ensure that the seeds grow well and that there is no danger to the people working in the fields at weeding time. This is an activity in which accidents are frequent, so people wish to minimize the danger through the ritual blessing of their activity.

First fruits

The first fruits at the end of the cultivating season are in many African societies regarded as holy or sacred. They open up the way for the ripening of the fields and the harvest. Therefore there are rituals to mark this consideration. The rituals take away any dangers that could be incurred in eating the new harvest. This idea may be thought of as 'cooling off' the crops, or blessing the harvest, tasting the food or taking away bitterness. The rituals of the first fruits are like religious signals to people that they may now safely eat the fruit of their labours, because by blessing the first fruits the whole harvest is consequently blessed and made holy (sanctified) or ritually clean for human consumption. The ritual also gives an opportunity for people to express their gratitude to God for the new harvest, and in many cases some of the first fruits are offered to him for that purpose.

Harvest rituals

Harvests are marked with a lot of festivals when people relax and begin to enjoy the fruit of their labours in the fields. They dance, they eat, they take it easy; and they rest from working so hard, which also gives the fields an opportunity to rest. In addition they have time to do other things while waiting for the next planting season.

Materials for rituals

Almost all types of seeds and all parts of both domestic crops and wild plants are used in one way or another for various rituals. Some are ground into powder which is mixed with other ingredients for medicinal and ritual uses; roots, leaves, stalks, branches, and flowers are used in rituals of purification and rituals for the prevention of harm, for blessing and so on. Seeds or beans are used in the rituals of remembering the departed, especially by placing them in domestic shrines. Diviners, oracles and medicine men use various parts of plants and crops for divination and medical practices.

Thus, through rituals people are able to link themselves mystically with the world of plants and crops. All these things are at the disposal of man to use physically for food and ritually for his religious life.

Stock-keeping rituals

The keeping of cattle, sheep and goats is widespread in Africa. There are many societies which live more or less on that alone. Livestock plays a very important role in the life of the people, not only for food but also for social and economic purposes. These animals are valued greatly everywhere, and there is a whole culture revolving around stock-keeping. Consequently many rituals are performed in connection with the keeping and use of animals.

In some places, such as Kenya, Tanzania, and the Sudan, there are people who value their cattle as much as, and often more than, their fellow human beings. They would even choose to die in the process of protecting or rescuing their cattle. They give personal names to their cattle, they sing to them, they talk to them, they take infinite care over them. Their whole life is occupied with the welfare of their animals.

Stock-keeping rituals include those of killing the animals, eating them, milking, selling and buying, blood-letting and drinking the blood, using the animals for purposes of hospitality and in contracting marriage. The purpose of the rituals varies according to the occasion. In killing the animals, the rituals are intended to bless the use to which the meat will be put, and to remove any danger or harm that would come from such use. If the animal is killed for sacrificial purposes, then the ritual will include blessing the animal, dedicating it to God or whoever is meant to receive it, and soliciting God's help as the occasion may demand.

Milking rituals

In places such as Namibia milking is done ceremoniously, and before the milk is used it must be tasted by the chief or other authorized persons. These rituals of milking and tasting the milk give a blessing to the milk, making it free from any physical and ritual harm, and thereby safe for human consumption. Butter or ghee from domestic animals is used in many parts of Africa for ritual purposes, in anointing the newly wed wife, anointing babies, anointing corpses for burial and so on, in addition to the normal eating or cooking purposes.

Parts of the animal used in rituals

Various parts of the animals are used for different rituals and purposes throughout Africa. The skin is used in Tanzania, for example, to wrap the corpse of the dead for burial. Animal horns are used for musical instruments, and more often for keeping traditional medicines and for divination rituals. The entrails or their contents are used in purification rituals, and sometimes for medicinal purposes. Probably the idea behind the use of animal parts for rituals is that the life of the animal is passed on to that of the people concerned, to strengthen or protect it. It is also another indication that African peoples do not draw a sharp distinction between human life and that of other creatures.

Blood-letting

Blood-letting is done in many parts of Africa such as Kenya, Tanzania, Uganda, Sudan, Namibia, Nigeria and elsewhere. The blood is used mainly as food without killing the animal. Since this means eating part of an animal which is still alive, there are rituals to preserve both the animal and the people, to bless the blood, and to increase the mystical link between the eaters and the animals. Some of the blood may also be poured on the ground as a libation for the departed, or as a way of blessing the ground to make it more productive.

Chickens in rituals

Fowls, especially chickens and sometimes guinea fowls, are used in many rituals throughout Africa. Chickens are found in almost every village. They are used for sacrifices on an individual and family basis. They are also used in rituals as may be directed by the diviner or medicine man, as part of the process for the treatment or prevention of illness. During personal rituals the chickens are either used alive or more often killed as part of the ritual. Their feathers, nails, entrails and beaks are often used in various domestic rituals.

Wild animals

Wild animals are used in rituals such as sacrifices for rain-making, in chasing away epidemics and public danger, and in purifying the land. Formerly human beings were also killed for ritual purposes. Even today one reads in the papers from time to time about the alleged slaying of people in order to use their bodies or parts of their bodies for rituals. It is also said in the villages that witches and night-dancers dig up graves to obtain parts of the corpse or skeleton in order to use them for rituals.

Thus we find that animals, including domestic animals, fowls, wild animals and even human beings are often in demand for use in rituals. The fact that their life has generally to be taken before they are used in ritual makes people feel that the ritual is a serious business and strengthens their belief in its effectiveness. Human life is in this way mystically tied up with that of other animals. But the fact that it is for man's purpose that these animals are killed shows how much man considers himself to be at the centre of creation.

• Health Rituals

In every society of the world, health is always a major concern. African peoples have many rituals directed at ensuring good health, healing, preventing danger to health, curing barrenness, removing impurities in people and homesteads, and protecting people, animals and crops.

Disease is not just a physical condition, according to African interpretation and experience. It is also a religious matter. Therefore to deal with it people revert to religious practices. They use religion to find out the mystical cause of the disease, to find out who has been responsible for it or has sent it to the sick person. They use religion to prescribe the right cure, part of which is often the performance of certain rituals that the medicine man may specify. It is also necessary to take counter measures to make sure that the cause of the disease is neutralized so that the person concerned will not suffer from the same disease again.

We said in Chapter 11 that the death of any individual is believed to have a cause. Therefore many rituals are performed in the villages to prevent death, to delay death, to ward it off. Even when it has struck, part of the funeral rites include the idea of chasing away death from the family. For this purpose, the homestead and its people are purified ritually, and this renews normal life in the village.

Rituals of blessings for good health and long life are numerous. Often they are performed by the older members of the family, and occasionally a local diviner or medicine man is called upon to carry out formal rituals if the family's health is in serious danger. Normally, however, communal health rituals are carried out for villages in a given area, especially if there is an epidemic. From time to time there are witch-hunting rituals and cleansings, to ensure that witches do not terrorize people or that their powers are kept under control. There are other rituals performed to drive away the spirits from troubling people. These involve whole communities, although they may also be carried out on a family basis.

Other health rituals concern women's menstruation, miscarriage and birth. Various taboos exist concerning these natural processes of the body, and for that reason rituals are carried out to enforce the taboos, to remove breaches against the taboos, to purify the women and what they touch, especially during menstration and after giving birth. Everything possible is done ritually to cure barrenness, and in some places all the barren women of a particular region come together for a communal ritual to cure them. Other related rituals are performed upon young girls and unmarried girls to prevent them from contracting barrenness.

We could even say that ultimately all the rituals that people perform are for the welfare of the individual and society. They are in effect health rituals since they are aimed at preserving and prolonging human life.

• Homestead Rituals

These are those rituals which concern life in the homestead. They cover the building of new houses and barns for storing food, the fencing of cattle sheds, entering a new house, showing hospitality to guests and visitors, the departure and return of family members when they go away from home, and rituals concerned with major changes in the family such as birth, marriage and death. For all these aspects of home life, African peoples have many rituals. The rituals are intended to bring blessings upon the homestead, to remove the impurities of sickness, to strengthen social ties, to define the duties and rights of different members of the family, and to make the life of the homestead run smoothly.

• Professional Rituals

These are the rituals which deal with the many activities for which a certain measure of skill and training is necessary. They are used in connection with hunting and fishing, the making and using of spears, bows and arrows, canoes, the trapping and tracking of animals, and the sharing out of the kill in hunting expeditions. Other rituals are concerned with formal professions such as those of medicine men, diviners, oracles, priests, rain-makers, ritual elders, blacksmiths, magicians and witches. Another category of people governed by special rituals is that of kings, chiefs, queens, rulers and other traditional leaders. For all these, there are rituals of every kind, intended to make sure that a high professional standard is maintained, and that good order and harmony are observed. Rituals help to reduce conflict and tension in various professions; and members of each profession are self-protected by the rituals they undergo, some of which force them to take oaths of secrecy.

In the case of rulers, many rituals surround the person and life of the individual concerned. There are rituals of accession, rituals

A team of men who run ahead to alert people that the Egungun masquerade is on the way, and that women should keep out of sight for this particular Egungun. Note the speaking drum and the man with religious objects (Nigeria).

of movements from one place to another, rituals of meeting other rulers, rituals of royal weddings, rituals governing what they may or may not touch, and elaborate rituals attending their burial.

In professional rituals there are many taboos concerned with what people may not do, what they may not eat or touch, how they should behave at certain times and how to carry out their profession properly. These rituals enhance the stature of their office and the effectiveness of their professional performance.

• Festivals

There are many occasions when festivals add to the grandeur of both personal and communal rituals. Festivals for individuals and families may accompany birth, initiation, marriages and funerals. In the life of the community there are harvest festivals, planting festivals, hunting and fishing festivals, victory festivals, coronation or accession festivals, and many others. In places such as Nigeria there are different types of festivals and masquerades to mark the return of the spirits to human societies, and to celebrate or renew the fertility of people and fields. They last many days. Sometimes more or less everyone participates in them, but sometimes women

A detail of an Egungun masquerade costume. This particular Egungun recalls the visit of spirits among people (Nigeria).

are not allowed to participate or even watch what the men are doing. These annual festivals involve wearing masks, dancing, feasting, making offerings and sacrifices, praying, blessing people, and general jubilation. Some of the most beautiful masks in Nigeria and other countries of Africa are made and used for festivals of this kind.

The benefits brought by festivals

Through festivals the life of the community is renewed. People are entertained, and their tensions find an outlet. Festivals also bring together the people as a group, thus strengthening their unity and cohesion. Religious and social values are repeated and renewed through communal festivals. Artistic talents are utilized to the full, in the form of art, music, drama and oral communication. Where the festivals involve beliefs concerning the unseen world, the link between human beings and the spirits is renewed and yet the two worlds are kept at a healthy distance from each other – dovetailing and yet neither interfering in the other. People seize such occasions to solicit blessings from God or the departed, and there is a general feeling that the visible and the invisible worlds coexist for the benefit of man who is at their centre.

Rituals and festivals are religious ways of implementing the values and beliefs of society. Without them African life would be dull. But for the modern man in Africa (whoever he is), there may seem to be too many rituals in traditional life, and the changing ways of living do not necessitate or allow for the observation of all these traditional rituals. Therefore many of them are being abandoned today. With that loss may also go the loss or weakening of the religious consciousness which governs so much of African traditional life. National festivals and celebrations are replacing some of the traditional festivals, but in village life there is still room for some traditional festivals in which everyone can participate wholeheartedly, spontaneously and naturally. Human life needs some relevant rituals and festivals to give it both solemnity and laughter.

13 • Religious Objects and Places

We said in Chapter 4 that African peoples consider this to be a religious universe. In the last chapter we saw the large number of rituals which are performed in connection with almost every aspect of human life. The African sense of religion entering all areas of life makes people feel that many objects and places have a religious significance. Some of these are natural objects and places, and others are made by people themselves. We have already come across some of them, but in this chapter we shall consider them together in order to see their value and place in African Religion. Some of the objects and places are regarded as sacred, but many others are simply used for a particular religious purpose and occasion, without necessarily being sacred or holy as such.

There are many beliefs, sentiments, myths and legends attached to these religious objects and places. This is what sets them apart from others. But beliefs and sentiments change from time to time, and then some of the objects and places are discarded or turned into common use once more.

• Personal Religious Objects

These are the objects normally in the possession of the individual for his private or family use. They are carried in a bag, or tied to his body (for example, to the wrist, ankle, neck or waist), or kept in the house, on the roof top, at the gate to the homestead, or in the fields. They include preparations made by the medicine man, objects used for rituals, bones, roots or branches of trees, certain stones, domestic utensils, and so on. Some are intended to ward off evil magic, others to discourage thieves from stealing, some are concrete reminders of the living dead, and some simply assist the person in performing religious rituals or saying his prayers.

• Ritual Objects

In the last chapter, we saw that there is a large number of rituals dealing with many aspects of life. For these, there are also ritual objects, which are used in performing the ritual concerned. Some are used by the individual or family, others by the community

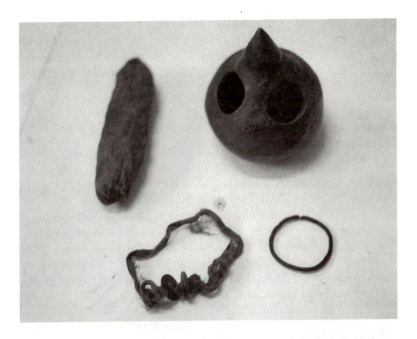

The gourd is used for marriage medicine, and is given to a new wife by the mother-in-law; the stick is used for religious rituals during pregnancy; the head-band is worn when one is speaking to or feeding the family spirits (living dead); the amulet might signify the bond of marriage, as it is given to the new bride on arrival, by her mother-in-law (Uganda).

under the ritual leader. Some are considered to be sacred, and hence very powerful. These are normally kept out of ordinary reach; and communal ones may be housed in the home of the ritual leader (such as the rain-maker, priest, or king). In bringing them out to the public and taking them away much ceremony is observed. They may include ritual drums, sacred stools like those used for the coronation of a new chief or king, rain-making stones (often believed to have fallen from the sky), masks for certain festivals and masquerades, and other religious treasures. For personal ritual the number is vast. Without them, rituals would not be as meaningful and impressive. These objects embody the beliefs attached to the rituals; they are the external concrete symbols of the internal ideas, beliefs and values which are demonstrated in the ritual.

Ritual dresses, masks, staffs, and other insignia are often considered sacred. People may not touch them under normal circumstances. They add to the stature of the office-bearer, whether he is a priest, king, medicine man or rain-maker. Therefore people take much trouble over making them. Certain colours and numbers which are used for religious rituals and ceremonies are associated with specific beliefs and ideas.

Ritual colours

The commonest ritual colours are black, white and red. These colours signify different things in different parts of Africa. For example, only black animals are sacrificed in certain parts of Uganda, Nigeria, Zimbabwe and many other places. Black for such people is the colour of purity and sacredness. On the other hand, elsewhere, black is associated with death, danger and evil. White animals only are sacrificed in other parts of Africa, thus signifying that white is the colour of purity and sacredness for those people. Yet there are parts of Africa where white is the colour associated with death, spirits, and evil.

Ritual numbers

Numbers also have their religious meaning. But different numbers mean different things for different peoples. For example, the number nine is sacred in certain areas of Uganda; animals and objects used for sacrifices must number nine. In Kenya, the number seven is considered unfortunate; therefore people try to avoid using it in their ordinary life. Yet in the same country, some people consider the number seven to be sacred, and in praying for rain they process round the ritual tree seven times and sit down on the eighth time.

• Objects for Offerings and Sacrifices

The many objects that are used for offerings and sacrifices automatically become religious objects. They are the concrete expressions of human intentions towards God and the invisible world. They show that, as the priest of the universe, man can and does use almost everything for a religious purpose. Through them the visible world penetrates the invisible world, and man symbolically presents or offers the visible world to the invisible world.

The items used for offerings and sacrifices are many, as we saw in Chapter 6, where we talked about how people approach God.

There are both domestic and wild animals, like cattle, sheep, goats, and a number of others. When these are sacrificed, being used for a religious purpose they become religious objects. There are also foodstuffs of every kind, which are offered in all parts of Africa. In some places, such as Nigeria and Sierra Leone, kola nuts are the most usual foodstuffs both for offerings and as an expression of hospitality. In Uganda coffee beans are similarly used. Every society has particular foodstuffs which are often used in religious ceremonies and for offerings.

There are other things such as money, beads, domestic utensils, old rugs, and so on, which people offer at shrines and other religious places. Once these are so used, they become religious objects. People do not necessarily have beliefs about these particular items. It is the intention and occasion of their use which make them religious objects.

• Religious Places

Every African people has its own religious places. They are not for common or careless use, because they are considered to be sacred or holy. Some of them are man-made and others are taken over in their natural form. Man-made religious places are those that have been constructed or adapted for the purpose of religious usage or for inspiring specific religious feelings. Natural places are set apart as religious places by common belief, practice and consent in the area concerned. In both cases the places are used for religious activities like praying, making offerings and sacrifices, and major ceremonies and rituals.

Man-made places

As a whole, African peoples carry out their religious activities in the open. But because the weather may be rough sometimes and some religious objects are difficult to move, people make specific places for religious purposes. These include temples, altars, shrines and graves.

Temples These used to be fairly common in places like Ghana, Nigeria, Tanzania and Uganda. Their numbers are decreasing, and in many cases it is hard to find them now. They are large buildings set apart for religious use, and looked after by priests and priestesses. Religious objects such as drums, spears, and utensils are kept there. In some areas kings, queens and other noble people are buried in these places. For this reason the temples also become places of pilgrimage.

Altars These are small structures on which sacrifices and offerings may be placed. They are often within other religious places such as shrines and temples, but they can also stand on their own in the open. They are reported to be still in existence in Zambia, Ghana, Nigeria and other countries.

Shrines These are the commonest religious places. They are found all over Africa. Some are private and family shrines, and others are public and communal shrines. Some are constructed in the form of small huts or mounds in the homestead or behind the houses. Graveyards of the departed are also used as shrines. Communal shrines are often natural places which have been turned into shrines. We shall mention them below when we talk about natural religious places.

Family and personal shrines are used for pouring libations, placing bits of food, performing family rituals, sacrificing and

Kola nuts are often used for religious and social purposes (Nigeria).

148

making offerings and saying prayers. They are the centre of family religious life. They symbolize the meeting-point between the visible and the invisible world.

Graves These are often treated as religious places. In some countries shrines may be erected on top of a grave, or the grave itself may be used as a shrine. Here the departed are remembered by pouring libations and placing bits of food there, and making prayers directed to or mentioning the name of the living dead in question, so that the departed may relay them to God or may receive the sentiments of his surviving family. The grave is cared for so that it is not overgrown with weeds. When the family moves the homestead to another place, it is the practice among some societies to dig up the remains of their living dead and remove them ceremoniously to the new homestead. In other cases, people retain the use of the plot of land where they have buried their dead. Such use gives them a mystical tie with their departed relatives. Graves as religious places are more important for farming communities than for pastoralists who are often moving from one place to another.

Natural places

Of the natural places used for religious purposes, there is no limit. Every society has many of them. They include groves and forests, trees, waterfalls and rivers, lakes, rocks and mountains. They are symbolically the meeting-point between the heavens or sky and the earth, and therefore of the invisible and visible worlds. People use them for rituals, ceremonies, sacrifices, offerings and praying. Such places are not put to common use; this would desecrate them. Where necessary, there are people who look after the general tidiness of these places. In any case there are ritual and religious leaders who take charge of any public use of these places, and see to it that they are kept in order where and when necessary.

These public religious places are the focus of communal faith, values, and sentiments. Almost nothing else generates religious sentiments as readily as do religious places. This is because people regard them as sacred and therefore as places where they feel the symbolic presence of God. Anything that seems to interfere with that belief is quickly resented, and may even produce a dangerous reaction from the people concerned.

Waterfalls often mark sacred spots, and religious ceremonies are conducted nearby. This is the Victoria Falls on the River Zambezi.

Groves, forests and trees Certain groves and forests are set apart for religious activities like rituals, ceremonies, prayers and sacrifices. For that reason, people do not graze their cattle there or turn them into fields for growing their crops, and in many cases they do not use them for hunting or cutting firewood. It is said in areas such as Kenya and Zimbabwe that if animals or people hide in sacred groves and forests, they may not be killed. Killing them would desecrate the sacred places and might incur punishment from God or the spirits.

Many types of trees are used for religious activities. Some are often associated with religious ideas, even if they are not always used for religious ceremonies, as, for example, the wild fig tree in Kenya, the baobab tree in many parts of Africa, and the silk-cotton tree (kapok) in Zaire. In Namibia there are people who believe that men originated from a mystical 'tree of life' (*omumborombonga*, botanically known as *compretum primigenium*). Although this tree is said to grow in the underworld (or to the north of their country), it also grows in reality on the ground. It is held to be sacred, and when people come across it, they greet it with respect as it is the symbol of life and continuity. We have already mentioned the ceremonial and religious uses of the kola nuts, so the tree from

Mt Kenya (Kilimanjaro) is believed to be one of the resting places for God when he visits the earth. Prayers and sacrifices are made facing this snow-covered mountain on the Equator Kenya).

which they come can be regarded as a religious tree. It grows in many parts of western Africa.

Rivers, lakes and waterfalls In many parts of Africa these are regarded with religious awe. People make sacrifices and take offerings there, as a sign of wishing to be in harmony with their waters, especially if they wish to fish in them or cross them. In some cases it is believed that there is a spirit inhabiting such rivers or lakes or waterfalls; therefore it is necessary to come to terms with it before using the lake or river in question. Waterfalls are used for religious activities because of their unusualness. In some places it is believed that the spirits of the dead dwell there. In that case people feel close to the departed through coming close to the waterfalls.

We should take note of the very common use of water in many rituals all over Africa. It symbolizes purification and cleansing, not only of bodily but also of mystical impurities contracted through broken taboos, the commitment of crime, and contamination by evil magic or curse. When so used, water becomes a religious object. Often such water is drawn from sacred lakes, rivers or springs.

Rocks, hills and mountains Places with rocks are also used for religious activities. This use of rocks for religious purposes goes back many generations, as can be seen from the large number of rock paintings found all over Africa. Some of these paintings depict ritual symbols, and others show animals used for food and sacrifices.

Hills and mountains lift people's eyes towards the sky, and hence towards God and the heavenly world. For that reason many of them all over Africa, including the continent's highest mountains, Mt Kilimanjaro, Mt Kenya, Mt Elgon, the Ruwenzori (or Mountains of the Moon), Mt Cameroon, and others, are natural religious monuments for the peoples who live nearby. Beliefs, myths and legends are associated with mountains and hills. Rituals, sacrifices, offerings and prayers are made on the mountains, facing the mountains, or at the foot of the mountains and hills in question.

To regions beyond the earth, African peoples have not been able to soar. If they could, they would turn even such spots into religious places. When Africans arrive on the moon one day, it should not be surprising if they use lunar mountains and rocks as sacred places, where they will pray to God for the welfare of our planet.

14 • Religious Leaders

• The Value of Religious Leaders

Religion has deep roots in people's lives. Therefore, to make it function properly in society, there are often men and women who have religious knowledge, and who know how to lead others in religious activities, and who serve as the link between their fellow human beings on the one hand, and God, spirits and invisible things on the other. We find many such leaders in all African societies. Their knowledge of religious matters varies considerably. Some of them are professionals, and therefore well trained and skilled. Others only take the lead when the need arises, otherwise living and working like ordinary people. Some are rulers and national leaders, and it is their positions which embody religious beliefs and emotions.

In many ways, religious leaders are the embodiment of what is the best in a given religion. They embody the presence of God among people and the faith or beliefs of the people, as well as their moral values. Without them African Religion would disintegrate into chaos and confusion. The religious leaders are the keepers of religious treasures and of religious knowledge. They are wise, intelligent and talented people, often with outstanding abilities and personalities. They include medicine men, diviners, mediums, seers, priests, ritual elders, rain-makers, and rulers. Not every society has all of these; and some of them combine two or more offices.

• Medicine Men

Medicine men are found in every African society and village. They may be either men or women. They carry out the work of healing the sick and putting things right when they go wrong. Their knowledge and skill have been acquired and passed down through the centuries. Since in every homestead and every village people fall sick or meet with accidents and misfortunes, medicine men are considered to be extremely important. They are the ones who come to the rescue of the individuals in matters of health and general welfare. Every homestead is, therefore, within reach of at least one and often several medicine men.

A medicine man, carrying medicine horns of bucks round his neck and medicine amulets (South Africa).

How people become medicine men

In some cases, children inherit the profession of medicine men from their parents. In other cases, a person feels the call to become a medicine man. This call or inclination may come suddenly or gradually. Where it comes suddenly, people say that they are called in a dream or through constant visits from a spirit, especially of a living dead. The call to become a medicine man may come to a person at any age.

A person then associates himself with a skilled medicine man in order to start training. This training can last up to ten years or even longer. It consists of learning the names and nature of herbs, trees, roots, seeds, bones, bird and animal droppings (excreta), and many other things which are used for the making of medicines. It also consists of learning how to diagnose diseases and people's troubles of every sort, how to handle the patients, how and what to prescribe as the cure, and in general how to perform one's duty as a medicine man. All this may be called the science of medicine.

Medicine men as healers

Major illnesses and troubles are usually regarded, treated and explained as religious experiences in African societies. This is where religion comes into the picture in the work of the medicine man. Minor complaints like stomach upsets, headaches, cuts and skin ulcers are normally treated with herbs and other medicines generally known to each community. But persistent and serious complaints require the knowledge and skill of the medicine man. Among other things, he has to find out the religious cause of such illness or complaint. The cause is usually said to be magic, sorcery, witchcraft, broken taboos or the work of spirits. The medicine man prescribes a cure which may include herbs, religious rituals and the observance of certain prohibitions or directions. The medicine man takes preventive measures, in addition, to assure the sufferer that the trouble will not come again. These measures also involve religious steps and observances. Therefore the medicine man serves as a religious leader, who performs religious rituals in carrying out his work.

Medicine men as counsellors

Furthermore, the medicine man acts not only as a doctor but often as a listener to people's troubles of all kinds and as their counsellor

A medicine man displaying a variety of his medicinal herbs (Kenya).

or adviser. When cattle die, their owners go to him for help; when children disobey parents, the parents go to him for advice; when someone is going on a long journey, he consults the medicine man to know whether or not the journey will be a success or to obtain protective medicines, and so on. Some medicine men are also the priests of their areas. They pray for their communities, take the lead in public religious rituals, and in many ways symbolize the wholeness or health of their communities. They deal in medicine, which means much more than just the medicine which cures the sick. It is believed that their medicine not only cures the sick, but also drives away witches, exorcizes spirits, brings success, detects thieves, protects from danger and harm, removes the curse, and so on. Medicine in African societies has a wider meaning, as we shall see in another chapter below, and these are the people who handle it.

Good and bad medicine men

The office of the medicine man is a very necessary and important one. Like other public offices, it can also be abused. Some medicine men use their knowledge and skills for the harm of society. But the majority are honest, kind, friendly and helpful men and women. For that reason people will call on them at any time of the day or night, and will pay any amount of money or property to get the desired help from the medicine men. People respect them, and some of them are highly feared because of the power of their medicines and spells.

Today we find many medicine men in or near the big cities. Unfortunately some of these have no training or skill as medicine men, and are only out to cheat their fellow men for the sake of quick gain. It may be necessary to establish government control over such pretenders, who earn a lot of money from selling useless articles and herbs, which they call medicines.

• Diviners, Mediums and Seers

Often this group of people works with the medicine men, and the same person may perform their duties and those of a medicine man. The main function of diviners, mediums, oracles and seers is to find out hidden secrets or knowledge and pass them on to other people.

Diviners

Diviners normally work also as medicine men. They can be either men or women. They deal with the question of finding out why something has gone wrong. They tell who may have worked evil magic, sorcery or witchcraft against the sick or the barren. They find out which spirit may be troubling a possessed person, what it wants and what should be done to stop the trouble.

For their work the diviners use divination. This is a method of finding out the unknown, by means of pebbles, numbers, water, animal entrails, reading the palms, throwing dice, and many other methods. It takes a long time to train in the different methods. Some diviners in Nigeria and Dahomey are famous for their knowledge of what is called the Ifa divination system, which involves a highly complicated arrangement of numbers and their interpretations.

Diviners, like other religious leaders, often have their own language. Sometimes they get in touch with spirits directly or through the help of mediums who often work with them. It is possible that diviners have a knowledge of how to use some of the

A diviner with his divination gourd (Kenya).

unseen forces of the universe. They also use their common sense and good imagination.

Mediums

Mediums are people who get in touch with the spirit world. They are often women, and they are attached to medicine men or diviners. They can get in touch with the spirits at will. But this is brought about normally by ritual drumming, dancing, and singing until the person becomes possessed, when she often falls down without being aware of it. Under that possession she may jump about, beat herself, bang her head, walk on fire and thorns, and do other things which she would not do when in her normal self. It is during such possession that she communicates with the spirit world.

Some mediums are possessed by only one particular spirit. They are said to be 'married' to it. Others may be possessed by any spirit. During their possession, they speak in a different voice, and some of them may speak other languages, which they do not otherwise know. The diviner, medicine man or priest who is in charge of the medium, is then able to interpret what she is saying. Most of the communication through a medium comes from the spirit world to human beings; people rarely have messages to deliver to the spirit world.

The medium tells where to find lost things, who may have bewitched the sick person, what types of ritual and medicine are necessary for the cure of people's troubles, whether an intended journey will be a success or not, which of the living dead may have a request to make and of what kind, and many other things.

Like other specialists, mediums must be trained. In countries such as Ghana and Nigeria there are schools for their training, which may last from several months to several years. Others are trained on an individual basis by priests, medicine men, diviners and other leaders. They may have a calling, like medicine men, or the parents may give over their daughter to be trained as a medium. In some cases, a particular divinity or spirit may ask for a certain girl or woman to become its medium for a while or indefinitely. If the medium is trained in a school, she lives with other trainees. Their training involves learning a new language, communicating with spirits, saying certain prayers, singing professional songs, dancing and the necessary exercises for inducing spirit possession. At the end of their training they are brought out in a big public ceremony, at which the relatives receive them with joy, presents and congratulations. They wear new clothes and often have new names and ways of behaviour. They then begin practising, normally in association with priests, medicine men and diviners.

Seers

Seers are people who are said to have natural power by means of which they 'see' certain things not easily known to other people. Sometimes they foresee events before they take place. On the whole there is no special training for seers. They are often people with a sharp capacity for both foresight and insight into things. It is also possible that some of them receive revelations through visions and dreams, in addition to being able to use their intuitions. In many African societies people tell about famous seers who predicted certain events like the coming of Europeans, the building of the railways, the flying of aeroplanes, and so on. Some of them no doubt make their predictions at the time when the events are just beginning to happen, when by the use of common sense they are able to deduce the logical sequence of events. Others have the ability to receive information through forces or powers not available to the common man. Seers may be either men or women.

• Ritual Elders, Rain-makers and Priests

Ritual elders

Ritual elders are the men and women who take charge of the performing of rituals in their community. There is no special training for this position. They normally occupy it through natural abilities of leadership and because of their age and experience. They are, however, well versed in the procedures, prayers, words, actions, intentions and times of the rituals which they conduct. Some of them are sons and daughters of previous ritual elders who began at a very early age to observe their parents carrying out rituals, and to learn from them by word and deed. Every ritual involving the attendance of a few or more people is supervised by one or more of these ritual elders. Therefore there are such ritual leaders in every village. For family rituals it is normally the oldest member who takes charge or conducts the ritual on behalf of the rest of the family.

Rain-makers

Rain-makers are, like medicine men, great friends of society. In some countries the office of the rain-maker is hereditary. The son or daughter of the rain-maker takes up the profession of his or her parent, and begins to train at an early age. There are both men and women rain-makers. Their position is often highly respected, and they may combine it with other forms of leadership, such as being rulers or priests at the same time.

Where rain-making is not hereditary, a person may be called to do it through dreams, messages from the spirits or a natural interest in the work. Training in rain-making is long. It involves learning to perform the rain-making rituals, to observe and interpret weather conditions, and to observe changes in the sky both at night and in the daytime, and the movements and habits of insects, birds, and certain animals, as well as the changes in plants and trees. All these things are connected with the weather, and nobody can become a rain-maker without knowing these fundamentals of his profession.

We find rain-makers all over Africa. Many of them are deeply religious people who spend a lot of their time praying to God to give rain to their people. They have a crucial job to do, since rain is the source of life for all living things in the country. In the Sudan they are called 'keepers of rain' and 'those who pray for rain'; in

Uganda they are called 'askers of rain', and 'those who cause rain to fall'; and in Kenya they are the 'seers or watchers of rain', or 'followers of rain'. Their duty is to ask for rain from God. They say that *they do not make rain*, they only pray for it, perform rituals for it, and as far as possible tell people when it will rain. Thus, they look to God to produce rain.

It is unfortunate that the English word 'rain-maker' has become so common when in fact it is so misleading. In many parts of Africa, God is referred to as the Rain-Giver, or Giver of Water. Furthermore, since the rain comes from the sky, people know very well that their rain-makers do not make rain. But the office of the rain-maker is important. He is there almost exclusively for the important job of pleading with God, praying to God to give rain to the land. In a few cases he may ask in prayer and ritual for the rain to stop, if too much of it is destroying crops and causing floods, or if there is an important event like a festival or wedding taking place on a particular day. Then the rain-maker is really the rain-stopper! But rarely does he do that, since rain is considered to be a blessing by African peoples.

Priests

Priests in African societies may be either men or women. Their work is to look after temples and religious places, to pray, to lead in public worship, to receive presents on behalf of God or other spirit beings, and in some cases to act as seers and mediums. They are also well versed in religious knowledge, in matters of myths, beliefs, traditions, legends, proverbs, and in the religious practices of their people. Traditional priests are found in Uganda, Tanzania, Nigeria, Ghana and other parts of West Africa, where people had or have temples and cults associated with major spirits (or divinities). In some societies priests are not found. Instead, ritual elders perform the priestly functions of sacrificing, leading rituals, praying, blessing and acting as the link between people and God. In some societies the traditional ruler is also the main priest of his people, and takes charge of religious functions.

The training of priests is done at the temples. Individuals may offer themselves to train as priests, but in many cases their parents send them to be trained. This happens if the parents have the feeling that God (or a divinity) helped them to get the child, or as an expression of gratitude for other blessings they may have received. In some societies women priests (priestesses) are regarded as being married to the divinity they serve, and until it gives them permission, they may not marry a man.

Training to become a priest involves learning various prayers, dances, songs, rituals, skills and crafts, and all aspects of their religion. After qualifying there may be a public ceremony to acknowledge their achievement or to initiate them ritually. When officiating publicly, they wear their priestly dress.

• Traditional Rulers

There are many African peoples who have or had traditional rulers. These rulers may be kings, chiefs, queens, rain-makers or priests. But there are many other African peoples who never had central rulers.

A lot of religious ideas surround the person and office of traditional rulers. In almost every society where they are found, their kingship or chieftainship is linked by myth and legend with God. It may be said that the first ruler was sent down from the sky by God, or was called or chosen by God to become king, or appeared mysteriously from God, and so on. For that reason the ruler has names of praise like 'child of God', 'son of God', and 'the chosen of God'. Such rulers have been or are still found in many countries of Africa, such as Ghana, Nigeria, Ethiopia, the Sudan, Uganda, Tanzania, Rwanda, Burundi, Zambia, the Republic of South Africa, Lesotho, Swaziland and Botswana. They are often spoken of as 'divine rulers', or 'divine kings', or 'sacred rulers'. The idea is that their office is believed to be chosen and approved by God, and in holding it they are like God's earthly representatives. Therefore they are in effect religious leaders. Their person, office and work differ from society to society, and there is no uniformity about them.

Rituals and symbols of the ruler's office

Many rituals are performed in connection with the person and office of the ruler. There are coronation and enthronement rituals and ceremonies; royal funeral rituals; rituals connected with the movement of the king or ruler, and with other activities such as hunting, going to war, eating, hearing court cases, receiving those who come to see him, and so on. There are also many taboos to protect the person and life of the ruler, and to enhance his stature.

Many symbols are used in connection with the office of the

ruler. Examples are the keeping of the sacred fire in the palace as a symbol of the nation's health, the use of leopard and lion skins as symbols of strength and power, the use of sceptres as symbols of authority, and royal drums which symbolize his ability to communicate with the people.

Traditional rulers in many societies are usually not easily accessible. Their palaces are surrounded by fences and guards. In order to approach them, one has to go through intermediaries. In many societies, it is even forbidden to watch the king eating and the king is forbidden to touch the ground with his feet or buttocks, otherwise he forfeits his position.

The ruler is a symbol of the people

The traditional rulers are in many ways the symbols of their people's health and welfare. They also symbolize unity and common tradition. They are responsible for the security and safety of their people. When they die, the land temporarily falls into a state of anarchy in some societies. These rulers are symbolically the representatives of God on earth, and sometimes the same terms are used of both them and God. Just as God is the king,

Royal drums, being played at the funeral of Kabaka Mutesa II (Uganda 1971).

An expression of honour and respect shown to the king or chief (Ghana).

ruler and governor of the universe, so these human rulers are the kings, rulers, and governors of their particular peoples. They exercise an authority believed to come from God. Therefore people are sensitive to what happens to their rulers, because symbolically these rulers are the heart of their people, and what befalls the rulers is emotionally thought to befall their people. Some of the rulers are also the chief priests, acting as the religious links between their people and God. In ruling they are performing not only political duties, but also religious duties. For many African peoples there is no sharp distinction between these duties. Consequently their political welfare is bound up intimately with their religious welfare. The ruler is there to safeguard, to protect, to enhance and to maintain that welfare. Therefore, people feel emotional about him, because he is the symbol of their health and life.

15 • Health, Magic and Medicine

• Enemies of Society

Perhaps the most disturbing element in African life is the fear of bad magic, sorcery and witchcraft. These are some of the greatest enemies of society. Every African people shares in that fear. Belief in the function and dangers of bad magic, sorcery and witchcraft is deeply rooted in African life, and in spite of modern education and religions like Christianity and Islam it is very difficult to eradicate this belief.

Witches and sorcerers are the most hated people in their community. Even to this day there are places and occasions when they are beaten to death by the rest of the people. Other human enemies are thieves and robbers who are also subject to communal forms of justice.

Other types of enemies are diseases, sickness, illness, accidents, barrenness, misfortunes, suffering, attacks by insects and animals, troubles from spirits, and above all death. Indeed death is the most devastating enemy, which comes at the end when other enemies have done their worst.

Natural enemies

There is a category of enemies which come through nature. These are drought, earthquakes, epidemics, famines, calamities and locust invasions. In their worst form they bring death to people, but more often a lot of suffering. These natural enemies attack the whole community. Therefore people more or less share equally in the sorrows they inflict. Generally no single human or spirit agent is blamed as being the mystical cause. In some places people reason out that God is punishing them for the wrong they have done.

In African villages many things are constantly going wrong. The enemies of society are always at work. The people ask themselves what or who has caused these things to go wrong in the form of sickness, misfortunes, barrenness, accident, death and so on. They believe that even if there are physical explanations of how an accident has taken place, which dog bit whom, and so on, there is also a major question of *who* made these things happen. Then comes a related question, asking how to put things right and prevent them from going wrong again. This chapter will try to answer these questions as experienced by African peoples in traditional life. The questions are raised mainly in connection with the enemies of persons and families; they are not raised to the same extent when it comes to the natural enemies we have mentioned above.

The answer to who makes things go wrong, is almost in every case a human agent and sometimes a spirit agent. This is where the matter of bad magic, sorcery and witchcraft comes in. We have already discussed the spirits. So here we shall concern ourselves with the problem of magic and related beliefs and practices.

• Magic, Sorcery and Witchcraft

When something goes wrong in the welfare of the individual or his family, he immediately wonders who has caused it to happen. It is not enough to answer how it went wrong. In most cases he will suspect that someone has used evil magic, sorcery or witchcraft against him or his household, animals and fields. This belief is found in all African societies. Once a person believes that someone has used evil powers against him, he goes on to establish the identity of the suspected offender. In most cases this offender is someone in the family, in the neighbourhood, or among relatives and associates at work.

We ask ourselves, therefore, what are magic, sorcery and witchcraft? When we considered African views of the universe in Chapter 4, we saw that people believe that there are invisible, mystical forces and powers in the universe. It is also believed that certain human beings have a knowledge and ability of how to tap, control and use these forces. Some have greater knowledge and skill than others; some possess the ability without knowing it, and find later that through word or ritual they can release these forces for particular use. Magic is believed to be these forces in the hands of certain individuals. They may use magic for harmful ends, and then people experience it as bad or evil magic. Or they may use it for ends which are helpful to society, and then it is considered as good magic or 'medicine'. These mystical forces of the universe are neither evil nor good in themselves, they are just like other natural things at man's disposal.

Witchcraft and evil magic

Witchcraft is a manifestation of these mystical forces which may be inborn in a person, inherited, or acquired in various ways. For some people it is said to function without their being aware of it, or having control over it. More often, however, it is believed that witchcraft and bad magic are combined and work evil whether deliberately or involuntarily on the part of the witch or magician. While we may look for a clear academic distinction between the two words, we have to bear in mind that in the villages there is often no such distinction. For our consideration here we shall treat the two terms, witchcraft and evil magic, as if there was no distinction between them.

Sorcery

Sorcery generally takes on the form of spells, poisoning, or other physical injury done secretly by someone to someone else or his crops and animals. Witches, evil magicians and sorcerers are the most hated (and often feared) persons in their communities. People fear to associate with them, to eat at their homes, or even to quarrel with them in case they may 'bewitch' them. In every African community there are endless stories and conversations about the use of magic, sorcery and witchcraft.

Methods believed to be used by witches

It is believed that a witch uses incantations, words, rituals and magic objects to inflict harm on the victim. To do this she may use nails, hair, clothes, or other possessions of the victim which she burns, pricks, or wishes evil to. The belief is that by inflicting harm on what once belonged to a person, that person is automatically harmed. Another method is to dig magic objects into the ground across the path where the intended victim is likely to pass, or at his gate, or in his fields. It is also believed that the witch may send flies, bees, other insects and certain birds or animals, to take harm to the victim so that when they touch him or he sees them, he will fall sick or meet the intended misfortune.

Another belief is that the spirit of the witches leaves them at night and goes to eat away the victim, thus causing him to weaken and eventually die. It is believed too, that a witch can cause harm by looking at a person, wishing him harm or speaking to him words intended to inflict harm on him. All these are the ways in which evil magic and witchcraft are believed to function. In some cases it is even held that powerful magic can make a person change into an animal or bird which then goes to attack the victim.

In every village people hold many such beliefs. No doubt some individuals also try to play the role described in these beliefs, hoping thereby to afflict their would-be enemies.

Motives for witchcraft

In most cases there has to be a reason why one person bewitches another. There are many reasons which bring about the use of witchcraft and magic. Often it is simply domestic tensions and jealousies that are bound to grow in any closely knit communities. For that reason, bewitching is reported mostly among relatives and neighbours. A stranger would scarcely bewitch another stranger. If there is a dispute between neighbours or relatives, one party may want to get rid of the other by means of mystical forces. Or, if something goes wrong following such a dispute and quarrelling, everyone will immediately suspect that it is caused by the other party through witchcraft and evil magic. Sometimes people may wish simply to get rid of others for the fun of it, or to inherit their property, or to take revenge for some wrong done to them.

Positive aspects of the belief in magic

While we may rightly condemn evil magic, sorcery and witchcraft, we should also see some positive points about them. Belief in these mystical powers helps people to find explanations when things go wrong. They are not satisfied with knowing only how misfortunes occur or diseases are caused. They want to know also who caused them to happen as they did, when they did and to whom they did. By putting the blame on the practice of magic or sorcery or witchcraft by someone in the community, people are able to reach an answer which appears to them satisfactory. Such an answer harmonizes with the view of the universe which recognizes that there are many invisible forces at work and that some of them are available to human beings.

Another positive aspect of the belief is that once people fear that their neighbour or relative may apply magic and witchcraft against them, they are likely to refrain from certain offences like stealing, rudeness, committing crimes, or deliberately offending their neighbours and relatives. Thus, the belief becomes a factor for stabilizing relations among relatives, neighbours, and members of the community.

We remind ourselves too, that those who may be suspected of

Statue of Queen (Dona) Sumba, wearing magico-religious objects (Zaire).

working witchcraft or sorcery or magic against others have their problems and that things also go wrong for them. They, too, find scapegoats in their communities. The whole problem becomes a vicious circle, and almost everyone is a suspect in the eyes of other people. This goes to show that those suspected of bewitching others are ordinary human beings with the usual good and bad qualities. They are not entirely evil, and only revert to the use of magic at times and for specific reasons if at all. They can also be cured of their evil practices, and each community has ways of cleansing or curing such suspects. Witch hunting and cleansing movements erupt from time to time in different African communities.

• Medicine

We have seen that when things go wrong people try to find the causes, and often these causes are believed to be human agents using magic, sorcery or witchcraft. People do not stop at only what and who has caused things to go wrong. They try to put right what has gone wrong, to heal, to cure, to protect, to drive away evil, and to counteract or neutralize the evil use of the mystical forces. To do this they use 'medicine'.

For African peoples, the word medicine has a lot of meaning. It

Various objects (claws, bones, feathers, shells, porcupine skins, etc.) on sale, for use in making medicines (Nigeria).

is unfortunate that in the English language it has a limited usage. Traditional African medicine is used for many purposes, one of which is to put things right and to counter the forces of mystical evil. There are, therefore, friends of society who are engaged in the positive use of mystical forces. These are chiefly the medicine men, herbalists, diviners, mediums, rain-makers, priests and even rulers. We discussed them in the previous chapter, so it is not necessary to repeat reference to their training and work. They help to stabilize society with their knowledge, skills and religious activities like prayers and rituals and sacrifices. They are the channels of good health, good fortune, fertility, peace and welfare. Their work is aimed at counteracting the many enemies of society we mentioned above. For that reason they are true friends of society and a public asset.

Medicine used against witchcraft

These friends of society are believed to have knowledge of mystical powers but to use it for the good of society. This we may call medicine to distinguish it from the wicked use of the same force which is witchcraft, magic or sorcery. A sick person is told by one of the friends of society not only who caused him to fall sick, but what needs to be done to cure him and neutralize the evil forces working against him. The medicine man or diviner gives him herbs, and often tells him to perform certain rituals. In addition to physical medicine he may be given mystical medicine which is believed to deal with the mystical causes of his troubles. These he may eat, dig into the floor of his house, place on the rooftop, carry about with him, or do other things with. The medicine man may even go to his home to apply his mystical medicine there as well in order to drive out the evil forces thought to be at work there.

Medicine used to bring good fortune

Thus, there is medicine to cure the physical conditions of illness. There is also medicine to cure the mental and religious causes of illness. There is medicine to prevent things from going wrong; and to protect a person or his belongings from being harmed. Other medicine is used to bring good fortune, success, favour, promotion, the passing of examinations and so on. People try to get these medicines and use them in various situations of life believing that they will thereby see their wishes fulfilled. Some use it to win the love of their wives or girl friends; some use it to succeed in hunting or carrying out business; some use it to find employment; others use it to protect themselves from meeting road or other accidents. I have even met a university graduate with an engineering degree, who used such medicine and claimed that if anyone shot at him the gun would not fire!

It is believed in many parts of Africa that medicine can be used by people to enable themselves to walk on fire, stand or lie down on thorns and nails, eat fire, fly through the air like birds, turn into animals, disappear and reappear at will without walking or using ordinary means of travelling, call up the departed and communicate with them, 'see' things happening away from the spot, and so on. I have not seen a demonstration of these powers, and I am only reporting what people say. It may be possible for some individuals to do some of these things, but precisely what powers and knowledge they use I do not know. The fact that most of us do not understand them does not mean that they cannot be done.

The use of medicine in this respect is limited to the activities of men. Natural calamities such as earthquakes, floods, droughts, famines and so on are not controllable or curable by human medicine. These are considered to be more directly under the control of God, and the most that people can do is to pray and sacrifice to him.

Medicine can generate a feeling of security

When used in the various ways mentioned above, and in many others, medicine generates confidence and a sense of security. Because there are so many occasions that bring pain to people, the world would feel very uncomfortable if there was no medicine to cure and counteract these endless experiences of sorrow and pain. Whether this medicine functions in every case or not need not matter very much. It is the belief in the efficacy of such medicine which inspires hope in the sick, confidence in the hunter and businessman, courage in the sufferer and the traveller, and a sense of security in the many who feel that they are surrounded by mystical and physical enemies. This in itself is a valuable benefit gained from the belief in medicine as African peoples understand and apply it.

Over centuries and millennia traditional medicine has provided treatment, cure, amelioration and other help to people, animals

172

and crops. It deserves to be given due respect. Herbs still provide direct or partial treatment and cure of diseases, as well as medical applications all over the world. Most of these herbs are in the tropics, and many of them in Africa. Traditional African doctors and herbalists have a treasure of knowledge concerning the medical uses of many such herbs. Some of that knowledge is shared and used commonly by people in the villages. Everything possible should be done to preserve and protect these and other species of plants from extinction.

The direct appeal to God

It is also believed that God is the ultimate source of all medicines. Therefore, people in desperation sometimes by-pass human dealers in medicine, and appeal to God directly for his intervention. They also appeal to him when all human help is exhausted. While bad magic, sorcery and witchcraft may symbolize evil in the universe, medicine symbolizes wholeness, goodness and health in the universe. These two function against each other and while evil may overcome individuals, goodness continues to maintain the wholeness of mankind.

African traditional societies and their religion found or invented magic and witchcraft to explain human experiences of pain and suffering and sorrow. They also discovered or invented medicine to cure and to protect themselves against these forms of evil and to promote health and welfare. These discoveries or inventions are the fruit of many and long experiences of life throughout the centuries. They satisfied people's search for explanations and solutions of their problems. They are still valid for many people in the villages. They need not, however, remain or prove to be valid explanations and solutions to the same problems for some of us and for those yet to be born. We ourselves may have to supply our own, and perhaps different, explanations and solutions in facing the same or similar problems.

16 • Morals in African Religion

• The Meaning and Value of Morals

Morals deal with the question of what is right and good, and what is wrong and evil, in human conduct. African peoples have a deep sense of right and wrong. In the course of the years, this moral sense has produced customs, rules, laws, traditions and taboos which can be observed in each society. Their morals are embedded in these systems of behaviour and conduct.

It is believed in many African societies that their morals were given to them by God from the very beginning. This provides an unchallenged authority for the morals. It is also believed or thought that some of the departed and the spirits keep watch over people to make sure that they observe the moral laws and are punished when they break them deliberately or knowingly. This additional belief strengthens the authority of the morals.

Morals deal with human conduct. This conduct has two dimensions. There is personal conduct, which has to do specifically with the life of the individual. For example he would ask himself whether it is right or wrong for him to eat, to work in his field, to visit the doctor or medicine man when he is sick, and so on. But the greater number of morals has to do with social conduct, that is, the life of society at large, the conduct of the individual within the group or community or nation. African morals lay a great emphasis on social conduct, since a basic African view is that the individual exists only because others exist.

Becauses of this great emphasis on one's relationship with other people, morals have been evolved in order to keep society not only alive but in harmony. Without morals there would be chaos and confusion. Morals guide people in doing what is right and good for both their own sake and that of their community. They help people do their duties to society and enjoy certain rights from society. It is morals which have produced the virtues that society appreciates and endeavours to preserve, such as friendship, compassion, love, honesty, justice, courage, self-control, helpfulness, bravery, and so on. On the opposite side, morals sharpen people's dislike and avoidance of vices like cheating, treachery, theft, selfishness, dishonesty, greed, and so on.

Morals keep society from disintegration. Even if the ideals in morals are not always reached, they nevertheless challenge people to aspire to them. They give a sense of inner peace to the one who observes them in his conduct within his community or among his associates, because he knows that he is not doing wrong or going against the accepted code of conduct. Many morals have become rooted in the life of the peoples concerned because of a long tradition of doing certain things and avoiding others. For that reason, some morals apply in one area but not in another, or at one time but not for ever. This is because of differences of culture, language, social structure, economic and political factors, as well as changes that take place slowly or rapidly in every society.

• Family Morals

Each person in African traditional life lives in or as part of a family. We saw earlier in the book that the concept of the family covers a wide range of members, including children, parents, grand-parents, uncles, aunts, various relatives on both the father's and mother's side, and the departed. Kinship is very important in all aspects of African life. Those who belong to one people (tribe) have a common origin and many other things held in common. The family is the most basic unit of life which represents in miniature the life of the entire people.

The rights and duties of members of a family

In the family individuals are closely bound to each other, both because of blood or marriage and because of living together. The moral order within the family must therefore be complete in order to regulate and maintain its welfare. In all African families, there is a hierarchy based on age and degree of kinship. The oldest members have a higher status than the youngest. Within that hierarchy there are duties, obligations, rights and privileges dictated by the moral sense of society. For example, parents have a duty to look after children, protect them, educate them, discipline them, clothe them and bring them up to be well behaved and integrated. These are the duties of parents towards their children. On the other hand, children have to obey their parents, to do as they are told, to work at home or in the fields, or as the older members of the family may instruct them, to respect those who are older, to be humble in the presence of their parents or other older people, and much later when their parents are old or sick to look after them. If parents fail in their duties towards their children, the wider community may punish them through pouring shame on them, ostracizing them, or even taking more serious steps. If children fail in their duties, they may often be beaten, or have something taken away from them.

At home it is expected that children will learn to tell the truth, to help other people, to be honest, generous, considerate, hard-working, friendly with one another, hospitable, and so on. These are fundamental moral duties which begin to be taught and practised at home.

The duty of hospitality

There are morals concerned with hospitality to relatives, friends and strangers. It is held to be a moral evil to deny hospitality, even to a stranger. Therefore, when people travel they may stop anywhere for the night and receive hospitality in that homestead. They should not be molested unless, of course, they abuse the hospitality they have received.

Other morals of the family

Other family morals concern property, the care of the home, the fields and the animals. People know what is right or wrong in their use of family belongings. For example it is wrong for a son to take his father's bull without his knowledge and to slaughter it or sell it. It is wrong to let cattle eat the crops in the field.

There are morals concerning the husband-and-wife relationship. It is held to be morally right that they should be faithful to each other, and wrong when either of them sleeps with someone else (unless custom permits such arrangements). It is held that they should care for each other, and each should do his or her duty for the welfare of the whole family without quarrelling or fighting all the time.

• Community Morals

Moving from family to community morals, the situation becomes more complex as it involves a vast number of people. Therefore there are many morals which govern the welfare of the community. What strengthens the life of the community is held to be good and right. What weakens the life of the community is held to be evil and wrong.

Taboos that safeguard the community

To safeguard the welfare of the community, there are many taboos concerning what may not be done and the consequences of doing so. For example, there are taboos forbidding the use of certain words which are thought to be offensive in various contexts. It is wrong to break those taboos, whether the taboos themselves are good or bad as such. Similarly there are tabooed actions, relationships, colours and numbers. It is taboo in many African societies for a person to marry a close relative. Breaking this taboo constitutes a breach of morals within the community.

Even though the individual exists for his society and not vice versa, the community respects his property and life. Other individuals would be morally wrong to molest him or steal his property. The community must show justice towards the individual, for this is a moral duty of society.

Morals of the whole community

There are morals concerning the social, economic and political life of the people as a whole. These cover aspects of life like mutual help in time of need, maintaining social institutions like marriage and the family, defending the land in time of invasion or aggression, protecting the children and the weak, punishing the offenders, maintaining peace, law and order, and so on.

Morals, customs, laws and traditions working together are the main pillars for the welfare of society. Morals produce and sanction the other pillars because unless something is felt to be right it will not become a custom or law. But in turn, when something is a custom, it becomes good and right in the eyes of society.

Good and evil moral behaviour

There are many things held to be morally wrong and evil, such as: robbery, murder, rape, telling lies, stealing, being cruel, saying bad words, showing disrespect, practising sorcery or witchcraft, interfering with public rights, backbiting, being lazy or greedy or selfish, breaking promises, and so on. All these and many others are moral vices in the eyes of the community. Whoever does them is considered to be a bad or evil person. The seriousness of the offence varies according to its nature, and from society to society.

On the other hand there are many things that are held to be morally right and good, such as: kindness, politeness, showing respect, being truthful and honest, being reliable, keeping promises, working hard, being hospitable, being considerate, helping others, looking after the homestead, practising justice in public life, keeping the good traditions and customs of one's society, and many others. Whoever follows these precepts is approved by society and considered to be a good person.

When people break moral laws, they suffer shame in the sight of society. In some cases they are ostracized or kept out of the social circles of their friends and relatives. In serious cases there are ways of making compensation and bringing about reconciliation. Sometimes rituals are performed to purify people who have committed serious moral offences, and to renew their good relationships with other members of their society. There was a widespread practice in many African societies, which has not died out completely, in which the community would punish a moral offender by beating or stoning him to death. This is done particularly to thieves and alleged witches. Such a step shows how seriously people take their morals, and that the community is above the individual.

In day-to-day matters of human conduct, people know what is right and good, as well as what is wrong and evil. They endeavour to do that which is good and to avoid that which is evil. The morals are normally written in their mind and conscience, through the long period of their upbringing and their observations of what other people do and do not do. Since the morals of each society are embedded in its customs, traditions, rituals, beliefs and practices, people assimilate them as they grow up and become participant members of their community and society. These are community morals, and everyone who is a member of the community must participate in its moral welfare. Whoever constantly or deliberately breaks his community morals eventually finds the community punishing him in return.

• God and Human Morals

We have pointed out the belief that God gave people their moral conduct. In some cases it is even stated which particular morals were ordered by God to be kept. God is thought to be the ultimate guardian of human morality. But people do not believe that he punishes moral offenders, except very occasionally. It is up to society to deal with those who break its morals. If society fails to find out who may have committed certain crimes such as murder, then the community concerned may pray or perform rituals to ask God to punish the unknown murderer.

Punishment by God for moral offences

In some places it is believed that certain diseases or accidents come only from God in punishment for unknown or unconfessed moral offences. If there is a large-scale natural calamity such as a serious drought, flooding, or a devastating earthquake, people often interpret it as a punishment from God upon the community or society concerned as a result of increased moral offences. This interpretation means that natural calamities are believed to be caused by society itself because of its falling moral standards. God brings these calamities to punish the people and bring them back to a proper observance of their morals. There are legends and stories in many African societies which tell how people were punished by God in the past for failing to observe morals and for falling into vice. The myths which speak about the separation of God and men, or of heaven (sky) and earth, and the coming of death, have often the same idea. In these myths everything would have gone well for men if only they had obeyed certain rules given to them by God.

The importance of good moral conduct

African peoples take the moral life seriously. Through myths and legends and beliefs, they show that from the very beginning men could enjoy happiness, peace, prosperity and well-being only if they kept the moral demands of human conduct. African religious beliefs, values, rituals and practices are directed towards strengthening the moral life of each society. Morals are the food and drink which keep society alive, healthy and happy. Once there is a moral breakdown, the whole integrity of society also breaks down and the end is tragic. There are, however, in every society men and women whose conscience fights against moral depravity so that through them and with God's help this tragic end of society is avoided and its moral life is renewed. Traditional African societies kept a close eye for any individual weeds in its moral life and often uprooted them before they turned human life into an immoral wasteland. In that exercise, the belief in God, the invisible world (with its spirits) pressing hard on our visible world, and the continuation of life after death, seem to have made a lasting contribution. Thus, African Religion emphasizes the importance of morals in practice, and insists that they must extend into all areas of life for the welfare of the individual and society at large.

17 • The Meeting of African Religion and Other Religions

• Africa as the Continent of Many Religions

In this book we have so far talked only about African Religion. This is the traditional religion of African peoples. But we have to remember that there are other religions in Africa. The continent is very fertile for religious growth. These other religions have originated from outside the continent, and some have won many followers from among African peoples.

Christianity

Christianity, the religion which puts its faith in Jesus Christ, came to Africa shortly after the death and resurrection of Jesus. It is believed in Egypt that Christianity was first brought there by St Mark, one of the writers of the Bible, in the year 42 A.D. Since then Christianity has spread to other parts of Africa and remained there. In the first six hundred years of its era, Christianity spread all over northern Africa, reaching as far west as the present Morocco. It also spread up the Nile Valley to what is now the Sudan, and to Ethiopia. Thus, by the beginning of the seventh century, probably one-third of Africa followed the Christian faith.

Ancient African Christianity

This ancient African Christianity thrived and produced many great leaders, thinkers and ideas in the Church. World Christianity benefited enormously from African Christians of the first six or seven centuries. This early spread and success of Christianity in Africa was largely checked or interrupted by Islam, which was founded in Arabia in the seventh century and which also reached Africa within a short time. But Islam in northern and north-eastern Africa did not completely wipe out Christianity from the continent of Africa. Ancient Christianity survived in Egypt and Ethiopia, where it is found up to this day. It is spoken of as Orthodox Christianity, to distinguish it from Roman Catholic and Protestant forms of Christianity, which are the other two main traditions of Christianity in Africa and which are historically newer there. In Egypt, the Christians belong mainly to the Coptic and Greek

Orthodox Churches, and in Ethiopia to the Ethiopian Orthodox Church. These three Churches have long and ancient traditions which go back many centuries. They also have accumulated treasures of Christian literature, art, ways of worship (liturgies), churches and monasteries. There are many ruins of ancient churches in these countries as well as in the Sudan and other north African areas.

Christianity in later centuries

In the fifteenth and sixteenth centuries, missionaries from Spain and Portugal brought Christianity to the coastal strips of western Africa and the mouth of the Congo river. There was a good response from Africans, especially in the kingdoms of the lower Congo. This lasted for about two hundred years and then died out. Similar efforts to establish Christianity were carried out on the east coast, but without lasting success.

During the nineteenth and twentieth centuries, much effort was put into bringing Christianity to the whole of Africa both by foreign missionaries from Europe, America, Canada, Australia and

A shrine of the Uganda martyrs, depicting the burning of many Christians at Nnamugongo on 3 June 1886, shortly after Christianity came to the country (Uganda).

181

New Zealand and by African converts themselves. In some places the response was slow at first, while in others it was quick and many Africans accepted Christianity. In Uganda, for example, within less than ten years after the arrival of the first missionaries in 1877, over 100 African Christians died as martyrs for their new religion. They were burned, clubbed or speared to death, and others had their heads chopped off. Other martyrs have died in Africa and Madagascar for the sake of the Christian faith, some as long ago as the second and third centuries. Many more have suffered and sacrificed themselves or their time and safety for the sake of the Christian faith in Africa.

Present-day African Christianity

In the present century, African peoples are responding very heartily to Christianity in spite of its having been associated with colonial rulers. By 1984 there were some 234 million Christians in Africa. Their numbers were increasing at the rate of about 5% every year. If that rate of increase is maintained, it is estimated by some scholars that by the year 2000 A.D. there will be roughly 400,000,000 Christians in Africa.

Although Christianity is spreading so rapidly in Africa in the latter half of the twentieth century, it is also facing many problems. In the minds of some people it is still associated with Europe and America, since it was from there that the majority of the missionaries came. But it must be borne in mind that Christianity is not a European or American religion. It came to Africa before it reached Europe; and it was already in Africa long before European and American missionaries began to preach it in other parts of the continent. So Africa has as much right to Christianity as Europe and America, if not more. The time has come, when now African Christians are taking impulses and new ideas of Christian life and experience to Europe and America, which could fertilize and enrich Christianity in those areas.

Divisions in the Christian Church

Another major problem facing Christianity in Africa is the large number of Church divisions, denominations, groups and sects. Many of these were imported from abroad. Many more were started by African Christians themselves, partly because they did not wish to remain indefinitely under the domination of foreign missionaries, partly because of personal wishes for power, partly because of wanting to make Christianity reflect African culture and problems, and for various other reasons. The widespread movement known as the African Independent (or Indigenous) Churches is now active in almost every country of Africa and Madagascar. This appeared first in Sierra Leone in 1819, but has proliferated to the extent that, in 1984 there were some 7,000 such churches, groups and religious organisations. They vary considerably in size, ranging from a few thousand members to several million members. In many ways they are attempting to integrate the Christian faith into Africa's cultural heritage and modern life situations. Nevertheless, the ghastly division of the one universal Church into these local denominations in addition to the many hundreds of other denominations coming from overseas, is not according to the teaching of the Bible and the will of the Lord, Jesus Christ. Therefore, the question of Christian unity is an urgent but also delicate issue in Africa, as it is in other parts of the world. Concerned Christians continue to repeat the prayer of Jesus Christ, 'that they may be one' (John 17:11), and work for its fulfilment.

Even though attempts are made to give Christianity an African character, its western form is in many ways foreign to African peoples. This foreignness is a drawback because it means that Christianity is kept on the surface and is not free to deepen its influence in all areas of African life and problems.

In spite of these difficulties, Christianity has made a great impact upon African peoples through its faith, its teachings, its ideals, and the schools and hospitals which have often accompanied the preaching of the Christian Gospel. It was in these schools that the majority of African leaders of today were educated. It is also by the Christian ideals of justice, human dignity, love and brotherhood that African leaders were inspired to fight against colonialism and foreign domination. It is through the same ideals that they still continue to fight against the remaining forms of colonialism, racism and exploitation. It is to be hoped, too, that those ideals will inspire the fight against tribalism, poverty, corruption, exploitation, unemployment and other ills which afflict independent African nations today.

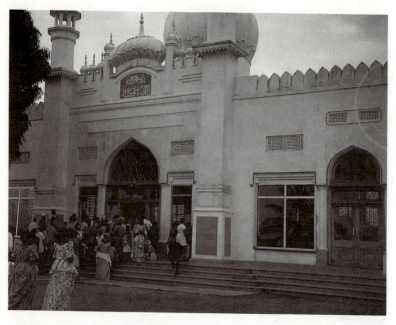

Wedding party entering a mosque (Uganda).

Islam

Islam is the religion that the Prophet Muhammad founded in Arabia early in the seventh century. His followers were persecuted, and some fled across the Red Sea into Africa where they were given shelter. Muhammad died in 632, and a few years later his followers began to spread into Africa. They came to conquer not by the doctrine of love which Christianity at its best teaches, or by persuasion, but by the sword. They swept across Egypt and north Africa within less than a century. Islam established itself wherever the Arabs conquered. The same happened in the Horn of Africa and partly the east coast of Africa. At the same time these Arab Muslims turned Africans into slaves whom they marketed, exported or used in their homes and estates, for more than a thousand years up to the present century. Shockingly, slavery has not yet come to an end. It was reported in 1989, that there are Africans enslaved by Arabs in some countries such as the Sudan! How long is the world to continue tolerating this form of injustice and brutality?

As it deepened its roots across northern Africa and the Sahara, Islam managed to wipe out Christianity partially in some places and completely in others. There remained a remnant of Christianity in Egypt; it was many centuries before Christianity in the Sudan died out, and Islam failed to conquer Christianity in Ethiopia.

Islam in present-day Africa

Today we find Islam dominant in approximately one-third of Africa, covering the Saharan region and north of it, as well as the north-eastern strip of Africa including the whole of present Somalia. There are strong Muslim minorities in some parts of Uganda, the Durban area, Ethiopia, Malawi, Mozambique and Tanzania. The greatest numbers of African Muslims are found in the west, in Nigeria, Niger, Senegal, Guinea, Gambia, Ivory Coast, Sierra Leone and Chad.

Like Christianity, Islam has its problems. One of these is the divisions and factions into which, like Christianity, it tends to fall. Another major problem is legalism. Islam has many laws which originated from the Arab society where it was founded. These laws are a major part of Islam, and though modifications and attempts to modernize them are made, Islamic law continues to exert great influence on the life of Muslims throughout the world. Government measures have been taken to introduce and enforce Islamic law (Sharia) in the Sudan, with all the injustices it brings upon Christians, followers of African Religion, and adherents of other religions.

Influence of Islam in Africa

Islam has played a notable role in the history and life of our continent. Muslims have been great traders, architects, philosophers and fighters (though the killing of other human beings cannot be praised by sane people, as being something 'great'). They traded for many centuries in ivory, gold and human cargo (slaves). They built towns and cities, especially on the Saharan fringes and the east coast. When Europe was in medieval darkness, Muslims in north Africa and the Middle East made advances in the sciences, philosophy and theology. When colonial rulers began to penetrate Africa, Muslims often accompanied them as interpreters and later as assistant administrators or civil servants, especially on the east coast of Africa. They also tended to be the ones who established trading centres along the colonial routes.

It is estimated that in 1984 there were 211 million Muslims in Africa. Their rate of increase is estimated to be about 2.5% every year. This increase is the same as the natural increase of population in Africa. At present there are only very few conversions to Islam, and nearly all the increase in the number of Muslims in Africa comes entirely from Muslim homes. Besides African and Arab Muslims, there are also Indian Muslims, their largest group being the Ismailis. These Ismailis are exclusively Indian and their sect has virtually no African members, giving the impression that it is organized on racial or ethnic lines.

Judaism

Judaism is the religion of the Jewish people. It is more ancient than Christianity and Islam. It produced Christianity, and shares many things with Christianity, especially the religious and ethical teachings of the Jewish Bible (which is the Old Testament for Christians). Judaism also influenced Islam and has some beliefs and practices in common with it. The Falasha people of Ethiopia are Jewish Africans, and live like ancient Jews as they follow Judaism. They have sacred scriptures, observe many of the laws,

An African Jew in Israel. In the 1980s thousands of African Jews (Falashas) from Ethiopia migrated to Israel. By 1986 there were 16,000 who joined millions of other Jews in the country.

186

customs and expectations of the Jews, and have ties with Jews elsewhere today. Many thousands of the Falashas migrated to Israel in the 1980s and 1991 and settled there. They experienced the process of being integrated into the country like other Jewish immigrants and similarly face some problems of adjustment.

There is a small group of Africans in Uganda who follow Judaism, particularly in those aspects of ancient Hebrews (Jews) which look similar to African life and practices. They are known as the Abayudaya; and the group emerged gradually after 1919, its early members having been Christians.

Judiasm is also found in other parts of Africa where there are Jews. These are countries like the Republic of South Africa, Morocco, Tunisia, Ethiopia, Zimbabwe, Egypt, etc. Jewish populations in north African countries which were conquered and occupied by Arabs used to be large but they have decreased as a result of Jewish migrations (mainly) to Israel since 1948, and the Arab-Israeli tensions in the Middle East.

Hinduism, Sikhism and Jainism

Hinduism, Sikhism and Jainism are the three Indian religions with followers in Africa. Their followers are all of Indian origin. There are practically no African converts. Like African Religion, these Indian religions can only be practised within the cultural context of their followers. They remain largely foreign religions, and if their Indian followers left Africa, the religions would also leave Africa.

Baha'ism

Baha'ism started in Persia in 1863 when its founder Baha'ullah made a proclamation of the new faith. It aims at uniting the peoples of different faiths, cultures, races, languages, and backgrounds into one. It lays much emphasis on equality, brotherhood and sisterhood, justice and unity. In 1911 the Baha'i faith was first proclaimed in northern Africa. Later in the second half of the century it began to reach other parts of Africa, and today its headquarters for Africa are in Kampala, Uganda, where there is a large temple built on a hill. A number of Africans have become followers of the Baha'i faith.

These are the main religions of the world which have come to Africa. Where they have converted African peoples, they have

The Baha'i temple (Uganda).

also met with African Religion. We shall now look at the meaning of that meeting. This is mainly between African Religion and Christianity or Islam, since these two are the other religions with the largest number of followers in Africa.

• The Meeting between African Religion, Islam and Christianity

Survival of African Religion in Islamic areas

Where Islam came and remained as the religion of conquering Arabs and slave masters, African Religion was gradually suppressed. But even so there are still traces of African Religion to be found in northern Africa, the Saharan region and Somalia. Where large populations of African peoples survived but were converted to Islam without having the long continuation of foreign political domination, African Religion also survived in stronger forms.

This survival of African Religion in predominantly Muslim areas is in the form of beliefs, rituals, magic and medicine. African traditional ideas and practices have been mixed with those of Islam to suit the requirements of the people concerned, so that they get the best out of both religions. Generally the people have adopted Muslim ways of dress and other cultural forms from the Arabs. But in matters of deeper things of life, such as birth, marriage and death, they have remained largely followers of African Religion adapted to suit their social environment. This is at least the case on the east coast of Africa, and parts of the Sudan, Nigeria and other regions of west Africa.

There are also areas where Africans have completely refused to accept Islam, saying that it is associated with the Arabs who persecuted them, oppressed them and turned their forefathers and mothers into slaves. A similar charge is made about Christianity in that it was associated with colonialists and racists. Naturally the ideals of these two religions are better than things which some of their followers have done to African peoples.

Today Islam no longer uses the sword to conquer African peoples. Conversions of followers of African Religion to Islam are extremely few. It is not clear why the spread of Islam in Africa has almost ground to a halt, except within Muslim families.

The spread of Christianity in areas of African Religion

Christianity is spreading rapidly in the areas of Africa where African Religion has been most predominant. At one time overseas missionaries and African converts condemned African Religion in the worst terms possible. But it is becoming clear that Christianity and African Religion have many features which do not conflict. It is upon these that Christianity seems to be building, in its rapid spread in Africa. African Religion and Christianity have become allies, at least unofficially. One has prepared the ground for the accommodation of the other.

African Christians seem to accommodate Christianity readily into their traditional world-view. This is taking place particularly around the notion of God. They give up certain ideas, beliefs and practices in their traditional life, and assimilate newer understanding of God's dealing with men as proclaimed in Christianity. They also acquire the vision of a new hope of men being reunited with God at the end of the ages. For many it looks as if the gifts which were once given to men but lost in the mythological past, are now to be regained according to the promises and hopes of Christianity. These are the gifts of immortality, resurrection and the making of all things new again. In this, Christianity seems to fulfil a great need in the African world-view which had no hope of rediscovering those lost gifts. There are many morals and ethics in Christianity which Africans find to be similar to their own traditional morals.

Parallels of Christianity with African traditional beliefs

The Christian idea of the Church has parallels with African traditional life in which kinship and the extended family play a central role. The Church is the Christian family, in which all are related to one another through faith and baptism in Jesus Christ. The Church also includes those who have died and those who still live. This is similar to the African view of the family of both the living and the departed.

In reading some parts of the Bible, African Christians find many aspects of ancient Jewish life which are similar to their traditional life. This makes it easy for them to feel that the Bible belongs to them and they belong to the Bible. At the same time there are new ideas in the Bible which enrich the people's understanding of the world as interpreted through the Bible and Christian teaching. In particular they see Jesus Christ as addressing himself to them and not only to the people of his region and time. His concern with the sick, the poor, the hungry and the oppressed, touches at the heart of African concern as well. People feel that he is concerned about them in their constant needs. They turn to him for help, and many African Church groups spend much time and prayer asking Jesus and God to assist them in the daily needs of their life.

Conflicts between Christianity and African beliefs

Yet we must also take note of the fact that there are conflicts between Christian life and the life of those who follow only African Religion. Part of the reason for this conflict is the large number of moral requirements demanded and put upon African Christians by their missionary masters. It is more of a clash between Western or European culture and African culture, than a specifically religious conflict. Some of the areas where conflicts arise concern traditional African rituals, especially those of offerings in connection with the departed, African initiation rites, marriage customs, the place of sorcery, evil magic and witchcraft in African life, and methods of dealing with disease, misfortune and suffering.

Some African Christians have broken off from mission Churches and formed their own where they are able more freely to incorporate traditional African customs into their Christian life. This affects the form of prayers, music, hymns, songs and festivals, and the attitude to dreams and visions, as well as the organization, which is modified according to the ways that seem to fit the followers best. Much of the traditional world-view is retained in many of these independent Churches. At the same time they are trying to make Christianity reach the roots of African life and bring hope where there was no hope. African Christians take Christianity seriously, adding it to the religious insights which they inherited from their forefathers, and applying it to meet the present-day needs of society. It is Christianity which gave them the courage to fight oppression and domination by foreign rulers, for it endorsed for them their value of human dignity and emphasized the love which should exist among all men.

• The Future of African Religion

We have noted that both Christianity and Islam have spread all over Africa. Islam has left traits of African Religion in the one-third of the continent where it is dominant. Christianity coexists side by side with African Religion in the remaining two-thirds of Africa. In some places the three religions rub shoulders, especially in the towns and cities of the equatorial region in both east and west Africa. Many people in fact follow a combination of African Religion and Christianity, some of African Religion and Islam, and a few of Christianity and Islam. Besides the effect of Christianity and Islam, we have modern changes which are disrupting traditional African life in every respect. The question arises now whether or not African Religion can survive for long.

African Religion will survive as part of African culture

It is probable that as long as African rural life continues, we can expect African Religion to survive there. At present about 70% to 80% of the African population is still rural. Therefore much African Religion will continue to be found among these people whose life is still tied to the land and traditional culture.

We said at the beginning of the book that African Religion is part of our rich heritage. It has influenced our cultures, and given African peoples their world-view. It is impossible for this rich African heritage to be completely wiped out even by modern changes. As long as there is a trace of African culture, it will also have some of African Religion in it.

Since something of African Religion finds a place in a major religion like Christianity, as we have mentioned, it means that certain aspects of it will be modified by Christianity and kept in the Churches of Africa. The same process is taking place, though to a lesser extent, on the fringes of Muslim areas, in societies where African Religion has been predominant.

African Religion moving into the towns

We should take note of the fact that African Religion is now moving into towns and cities in certain forms. Already traditional medicines are being sold there, and many traditional medicine men and diviners are reported to be doing prosperous business in towns. In Nigeria and Ghana, for example, many traditional festivals are still observed in towns and trading centres. Thus, certain features of African Religion are being carried out in urban areas; and often urban people revert to traditional methods of solving problems and responding to moments of crisis.

The fading of some aspects of African Religion

Obviously some aspects of African Religion will die out, partly through modern education, and partly because of the people's movement to live in the cities. But we need to remember that African Religion is complex, and even if certain aspects of it die out, other aspects will survive and many of them will be changed or transformed to meet the needs of the changing times. African Religion embodies a whole world-view, inherited from many generations past. It cannot all collapse in a short time. It has produced African peoples as they were when they entered the twentieth century, together with their cultures, languages, occupations, aspirations and problems. Some of the problems it tried to solve or understand still remain human problems, especially those concerned with birth, marriage, death, the hereafter, suffering, sickness, and so on. It will, therefore, continue to have something to say on these issues of human life, even if other religions such as Christianity and Islam, and scientific ways of thought, have come upon African peoples. African Religion does not seek to compete with the other religions or with science; it only wants to cooperate in the search for a better understanding of the world in which mankind lives, and in working for the welfare of all peoples.

We cannot say that African Religion is better or worse than these other religions. It is simply the religious system which Africans developed in response to their life's situations. Up to a point it gave them satisfactory answers to their problems, quenched their religious thirst, and helped them to find an integrated and meaningful interpretation and understanding of the universe. But these problems are not static, and the need for understanding the universe is not static. Man is forever expanding his horizon of knowledge and understanding. African Religion has contributed to that ever-expanding horizon. No doubt it will continue to contribute something but without ever pretending to supply all the answers for all people at all times. Every way of thought has its own limitations; and it would be completely wrong for anyone to stretch African Religion beyond those limitations.

18 · The Value of Religion

• Religion and Society

We now come to the concluding chapter of this book. In this last chapter we shall raise only one question and try to answer it briefly. The question is: what is the value of religion? This question must be raised for several reasons.

People find religion a necessary part of life

Religion is a universal part of human life. It must, therefore, have a great and important value, otherwise by now most people in the world would have abandoned it completely. In the case of African Religion, with which we have been most concerned in this book, we have seen that it goes all the way back into African history. It is as if African peoples do not know how to live without religion.

People are ready to spend their wealth on religion

People spend a lot of their time and wealth on religion. Some of the most beautiful buildings in the world are or have been religious buildings such as tombs, temples, cathedrals, churches, mosques and other sacred places. In many cities and towns of Africa we find these buildings, some of which have rich treasures of goods and historical objects. Religion must have a great value to people, otherwise they would not continue to spend so much time and wealth in putting up religious buildings, and making and buying so many religious objects.

People are often ready to die for their religion

People are often ready to die for their religion, and many thousands have done so. Many others sacrifice their fame, power, wealth, property and time for the sake of religion. Religion must have a great value for people, otherwise nobody would die for it or give so much for its sake.

Cicatrization marks on the stomach, probably given at initiation.

People sacrifice the best they have for religion

People make sacrifices and offerings of the best they have for the sake of religion. We saw that in African Religion even human beings are sometimes killed or sacrificed because of people's beliefs and practices. Therefore, religion must be even more valuable to them than the life of individuals or people's property.

People are ready to fight for their religion

Followers of a given religion are often ready to fight and defend it or something related to it. They are sometimes unreasonable, fierce and fanatical if their religion is threatened by force or disrespect. They treasure their religion, and anything that threatens it would seem to threaten their whole existence.

People carry out religious duties freely

From time to time, people go freely to perform their religious duties, ceremonies and rituals. They even fast, inflict pain on their bodies, deny themselves the pleasures and comforts of this life, go on pilgrimage at great expense, cross national boundaries and oceans in order to take the religious message to other people, and do other things, all for the sake of religion. These are done voluntarily, freely, willingly and happily in most cases, even though occasionally force or pressure may be put on people. People often decide freely to join a particular religion. It must be, therefore, that there is something valuable in religion to make people do all these things of their own will.

Governments see the value of religion

Most governments and countries of the world provide for religious freedom. This provision is often a part of their constitutions. People in these countries have the right to freedom of conscience, freedom of creed, freedom of association for religious purposes, and freedom of worship. Therefore those who make the laws and constitutions of the nations of the world must appreciate the value of religion. As far as is known, all African countries allow religious freedom to some extent.

Public holidays are associated with religion

In many countries of Africa, and the world for that matter, there are national religious holidays such as Christmas, Good Friday and Easter, the Muslim feast which ends the month of fasting, and so on. About half, and in some cases more than half, of the public holidays in African countries are associated with religious festivals.

All these reasons show us why we must ask the question of the value of religion in human life. There are several answers to this question. We shall consider the answers in particular connection with African Religion, but they also apply to other religions in general.

• Religion Cultivates the Whole Person

People apply their religion to their social, emotional, economic, intellectual and spiritual life. They believe that religion is relevant in all these areas of their life. In the case of African Religion, which enters all aspects of life, it has been responsible in traditional African life for cultivating the whole person.

• Religion Provides People with a View of the World

When in Chapter 4 we looked at African views of the universe, we saw that they are deeply religious. Therefore religion has given African peoples a way of understanding the world in which they live. This is important, because that understanding of the world affects their experience of life. It supplies them with answers to the questions which arise for all human beings. To say this does not mean that they are the correct or the only answers. They are simply answers which people have found practicable and meaningful to themselves. People cannot live without asking questions about their existence and the existence of the world, and about their own experiences of being alive.

African peoples have found answers to these questions within their African Religion, even if some of the questions may not be satisfactorily answered. By giving people a way of interpreting the world, a way of understanding their own existence, African Religion has equipped them emotionally, intellectually and culturally to go through life and face its many experiences. If what gives them answers and solutions was suddenly abolished, people would feel lost in this vast universe. Religion acts as a light and guide to people as they go through life and reflect upon it.

• Religion Answers Some Questions which Nothing Else Can Answer

Today science has become the main source of our knowledge of the physical universe. But for all its great contribution to human knowledge and learning, science has its own limitations. There are questions which it cannot answer. For example, the question of whether or not God exists, the question of suffering and pain in the world, the problem of what happens after death and the destiny of the soul, the question of the purpose of human life, and so on. These questions are left to religion to answer, and sometimes philosophy helps in supplying answers. But most people in the world cannot understand philosophy or science, whereas almost everyone is able to follow or obtain something from religion. It is religion, therefore, which tries to solve these profound questions for everyone. Without it we certainly would be more ignorant than we are concerning these and many other problems.

• Religion Provides Mankind with Moral Values by which to Live

Part of any religious system is its moral values which regulate and harmonize human life. It is religion which tells us what is right and what is wrong, what is good and what is evil, what is just and what is unjust, what is a virtue and what is a vice. We saw that African Religion has many moral values within the family and within the community. No society can exist without morals. Religion enriches people's morals, for the welfare of the individual and society at large. It is morals which build relationships between people and between them and the world around.

• Religion Gives Food to meet Spiritual Hunger

In many religions of the world, including African Religion, it is recognized that people have both physical and spiritual parts. It is only religion which nourishes the spiritual part of man. That does not mean that religion ignores the physical side. In fact true religion is concerned with both the physical and spiritual welfare of man. To feed the spiritual half of man, religion provides spiritual insights, prayers, rituals, ceremonies, sacrifices and offerings, dedication, devotion, trust in God, and other religious exercises.

We saw that African Religion has many rituals of every kind. These are the channels for the contact between men and the spiritual world, between men and God. Through them men stretch out their spiritual parts towards the invisible world and the things of the spirit. This spiritual hunger for peace, joy, comfort, security, hope, love and so on, can only be satisfied by religion.

• Religion has Inspired Great Ideas

We have said that African Religion has provided throughout the centuries the answers to the problems which people faced. It has also inspired the great ideas of our peoples concerning, for example, the moral life (courage, love, endurance, helpfulness, sense of kinship, and so on), cultural achievements (music, art, carving, dance and architecture), social organizations and institutions (such as the family, marriage, kinship, clans and age sets), political systems (such as the idea of divine rulers which we discussed in an earlier chapter), and the building of the past civilizations of our peoples.

Some of these great ideas passed unrecorded, because many of our peoples did not use the art of writing; but the little information and evidence which remain show that religion inspired them to do great things, to build great cities, to accomplish great works of art, and so on. Some of the ideas have been handed down through various skills and traditions. Without religion our history would have been greatly impoverished. The same applies to the history of other countries, where other religions like Christianity, Islam, Hinduism, Shintoism, and so on, have influenced the thinking and living of people. Religion inspires people to produce the best, the greatest, and the noblest that is in them.

• Religion as a Means of Communication

Religion helps people to communicate in two directions. First, there is social communication. People meet together for a common purpose, for example to pray together, to perform a ritual together, to sacrifice together, and so on. They also meet indirectly through having common myths, legends, values, traditions, morals and views of the world. Because of religion they are able to understand one another, to communicate ideas and feelings and to act more or less as a social unit, even if there may be other differences. At least in theory, religion gathers people together both in action and in religious commitment. This can be thought of as the horizontal direction of religious communication.

Secondly, there is vertical communication between man and God, as well as between man and the spirit beings. We saw that African peoples are very much aware of the invisible world, which is an essential dimension of their views of the universe. These two worlds are close to each other. Therefore African peoples feel that they have to communicate with that invisible world as well. It is religion which turns their life in that direction so that they can communicate with God, with the spirits and particularly with the living dead who form part of their family. They are also able to penetrate the forces and powers of nature, which often they imagine to be personal forces.

• Religion Pays Attention to Key Moments in the Life of the Individual

We saw that African Religion marks through ritual and ceremony many of the key moments in the life of the individual, particularly birth, initiation and puberty, marriage and death. This shows that religion recognizes the value of the individual, since it is individuals who make up the community. African Religion tells the individual at these moments that he exists because of the community. Therefore the community celebrates these key points in the life journey of the individual. In doing so the community is renewing its own life, and re-living the cycle of its own existence. It is also religion which reminds the individual, through these ceremonies, that at death his life will not terminate, and that someone will remain to remember him, to keep him among the living, and to welcome him into the wider family.

• Religion Celebrates Life

African Religion affirms life, and celebrates life. We saw the large numbers of rituals, festivals and ceremonies which are carried out in African Religion. These all add up to the celebration of life. People know that they are alive. They want to celebrate the joy of living. They do not sit down meditating upon life. Instead, they put it into action: they dance life, they sing life, they ritualize life, they drum life, they shout life, they ceremonize life, they festivize life, for the individual and for the community.

African Religion does not promise people a better life in the future or in the hereafter. Those who have departed do not go either to a better place or to a worse place than this present life. Instead, it says that this is the time to celebrate life both in joy and in sorrow.

But even if African Religion asserts this life, it does not mean that people must go wild in trying to get the most out of it. Life is well regulated to ensure that all have the right to live and to join in the celebration of that life. According to African Religion, there is no end of the world, for human life goes on and on. Man is at the centre of the universe, created and placed there by God. It is the same God who is the ultimate guardian of human life both physically and morally.

In some religions of the world, there is an idea of salvation for which their followers must strive. This is not so with African Religion. Its main contribution is to make people deeply sensitive to the invisible world which dovetails with the physical world, and to help them to communicate both horizontally with one another and vertically with God and the invisible world. This is the ideal structure of African Religion, but its details are many and varied.

• Religion Shows People their Limitations

Probably the greatest value of religion is to teach people to be humble because of their great limitations. It tells men that they are created, and that however much they may celebrate this life, it is short, temporary and flowing like a river. Religion teaches men to be dependent on their Creator. Even though African Religion puts men at the centre of the universe, it also shows them very clearly that they have their limitations. This is what drives them to their rituals, prayers, ceremonies and trust in God. Even the greatest achievement of man is limited, and does not last for ever.

Whether religion is right or wrong, it tells men to be humble in the sight of their Creator who is God, and to trust in him. Their life comes from him and depends on him. In directing people to put their trust in God, religion is doing the best it can for men, by showing them both their origin and their destination. This is what, in its own limited ways, African Religion has done for African peoples throughout their history.

Appendix A · Questions

Chapter 1: The African heritage
1. Describe three types of African heritage, and indicate why you think that they are important.
2. What is the meaning of culture?
3. Collect or make a list of twenty African proverbs from any African people. Show their meaning and the context in which each is used.

Chapter 2: What is African Religion?
1. What are the five essential parts of African Religion?
2. Why is it not possible to win converts to African Religion from peoples who are not African?
3. What is meant by the statement that, 'African Religion is practised more on a communal than an individual basis'?
4. List four ideas about African Religion, and show why they are, or are not, wrong.

Chapter 3: Where African Religion is found
1. Enumerate five areas of life where African Religion is found, and elaborate on any two of them.
2. In what ways are beliefs important for the daily life of individuals?
3. Describe the geographical distribution of African Religion on the continent of Africa and the island of Madagascar.

Chapter 4: African views of the universe
1. Discuss the origin and nature of the universe according to African views.
2. Describe four types of order believed to be at work in the universe.
3. What is the place of man in the universe?

Chapter 5: Belief in God
1. Explain how the belief in God may have originated.
2. Give an account of the works of God.
3. What do African peoples consider to be the nature of God?
4. Discuss the value of human images of God.

Chapter 6: How God is approached by people
1. What is the meaning of worship?
2. Elaborate on any two ways by means of which African peoples approach God.
3. Who are the intermediaries between God and man, and what is their purpose in religious life?
4. Discuss the content and purpose of African prayers.

Chapter 7: The spirits
1. Give an outline of types of spirits, according to African Religion.
2. What are the differences between 'nature spirits' and 'human spirits'?
3. Narrate a folk story from an African people, in which spirits are used as a literary device to comment on human life.
4. Mention and explain three things which spirits are believed to do to people in a given African society known to you.

Chapter 8: The origin and early state of man
1. Explain (a) the meaning of myth; and (b) the value of myths in African life.
2. Give one African creation myth known to you, and attempt an interpretation or explanation of the myth.
3. Describe the type of life led by the first men according to African myths narrated about it.

Chapter 9: Birth and time of youth
1. Describe the traditional rituals performed at the birth of a baby, in any African society known to you, and show their religious meaning or purpose.
2. African names of people have meanings. Draw up a list of ten religious names and indicate their meanings or the reasons for their use.
3. What is the importance of initiation in African societies?

Chapter 10: Marriage and family life
1. Why is it considered necessary by African peoples for everyone to get married under normal circumstances?
2. Explain five meanings and purposes of marriage according to African views.
3. What is the value of children in an African family according to traditional views?

Chapter 11: Death and the hereafter

1. Tell one myth about the coming of death to the world, and explain its meaning.
2. What are the causes of actual death, according to African peoples?
3. Describe the funeral rites performed in any African society, and indicate the reasons for their observance.
4. African peoples believe that human life continues after death. What ideas do they hold about this belief?
5. What is meant by 'the destiny of the soul'? What ideas does African Religion teach about it?

Chapter 12: Rituals and festivals

1. Name four personal rituals and show their importance in the life of the individual.
2. Describe any two agricultural rituals performed in an African society known to you, and show their meaning for the people concerned.
3. What is the value of religious festivals?

Chapter 13: Religious objects and places

1. Describe some religious objects used in any African society with which you are familiar.
2. Briefly describe any three of the following religious places if they are known to you: a temple, a shrine, a sacred grove, a tree used for religious ceremonies, a sacred mountain, river or lake.
3. What is the value of religious objects and places?

Chapter 14: Religious leaders

1. Describe the training and work of either the medicine man or the rain-maker, in any African people known to you.
2. Mention four types of religious leader, and briefly discuss two of them indicating their significance or importance in society.
3. In what ways do African peoples regard their traditional rulers (kings, queens or chiefs) as being connected with God?

Chapter 15: Health, magic and medicine

1. Enumerate and comment on some of the things believed to be caused by the use of bad magic.
2. Discuss the good and evil effects of the belief in the existence and functions of evil magic, sorcery and witchcraft.
3. Elaborate on the wide meaning of 'medicine' in the African context.
4. Mention and elaborate on four ways of contracting the disease AIDS and four ways of preventing it.

Chapter 16: Morals in African Religion
1. What is the value of morals in society?
2. Enumerate six moral evils and show why people consider them to be bad.
3. Who is a good person in the eyes of an African society known to you?

Chapter 17: The meeting of African Religion and other religions
1. Strictly speaking, Christianity is not a foreign religion in Africa. Discuss this statement.
2. What problems is Christianity facing in Africa today? Suggest some possible solutions to them.
3. In what ways is Christianity contributing to the life of African peoples in the twentieth and twenty-first centuries?
4. What methods has Islam used to obtain followers among African peoples?
5. Discuss some of the problems facing Islam in Africa today.
6. Why have Indian religions failed to make converts among Africans?
7. What problems arise from the meeting between either (a) Christianity and African Religion, or (b) Islam and African Religion?
8. Is there a future for African Religion? Justify your answer.

Chapter 18: The value of religion
1. What leads one to think about the value of religion?
2. Which public holidays in your country are for marking religious events? Describe how religious bodies commemorate two of these holidays.
3. What is meant by 'spiritual hunger'? In what ways does religion supply food for it?
4. Describe how one religion, which you know or which you have accepted, pays attention to key moments in your life.
5. In what ways is religion a means of communication?

Appendix B · Books for advanced reading on African Religion

Note that some of these books also have their own select bibliographies for further reading.

Abrahamsson, H.   *The Origin of Death*, Uppsala 1951.

Awolalu, J. O. and Dopamu, P. A.   *West African Traditional Religion*, Ibadan 1979.

Beier, U., ed.   *The Origin of Life and Death*, Heinemann, London 1966.

Booth, N. S. ed.   *African Religions: a Symbosium*, New York 1977.

Byaruhanga-Akiiki, A. B. T.   *Religion in Bunyoro*, Nairobi 1982.

Danquah, J. B.   *The Akan Doctrine of God*, Lutterworth, London 1944.

Evans-Pritchard, E. E.   *Nuer Religion*, Clarendon Press, Oxford 1956.

Field, M. J.   *Religion and Medicine of the Ga People*, Clarendon Press, Oxford, 1937.

Forde, D., ed.   *African Worlds*, Oxford University Press, London 1954.

Fortes, M. and Dieterlen, G., eds.   *African Systems of Thought*, Oxford University Press, London 1965.

Harjula, R.   *God and the Sun in Meru Thought*, Helsinki and Arusha 1969.

Idowu, E. B.   *Olodumare: God in Yoruba Belief*, Longman, London 1962.

Idowu, E. B.   *African Traditional Religion*, SCM Press, London 1973.

Karamaga, A.   *Dieu au pays des mille collines*, Lausanne 1988.

Karp, I. and Bird, C. S., eds.   *Explorations in African Systems of Thought*, Bloomington (USA) 1980.

King, N. Q.   *Religions of Africa*, Harper and Row, New York 1970.

King, N. Q.   *African Cosmos*, Belmont (California) 1986.

Lienhardt, G.   *Divinity and Experience: the Religion of the Dinka*, Clarendon Press, Oxford 1961.

Lugira, A. M.   *Ganda Art*, Osasa Publications, Kampala 1971.

Mbiti, J. S.   *African Religions and Philosophy*, Heinemann, London; Doubleday, New York 1970. 2nd Ed., Heinemann, Oxford and Portsmouth (USA), 1990.

Mbiti, J. S.   *Concepts of God in Africa*, SPCK, London and Praeger, New York 1970.

Mbiti, J. S.   *Love and Marriage in Africa*, Longman, London, 1973.

Mbiti, J. S.   *The Prayers of African Religion*, SPCK, London 1975, Orbis, New York 1976.

Middleton, J. *Lugbara Religion*, Clarendon Press, Oxford 1960.

Mugambi, J. and Kirima, N. *The African Religious Heritage*, Nairobi 1976.

Mulago, V. *La Religion traditionelle des bantu et leur vision du monde*, 2nd edn., Kinshasa 1980.

Nadel, S. F. *Nupe Religion*, Clarendon Press, Oxford 1954.

Olupona, J. K., ed. *African Traditional Religion in Contemporary Society*, New York 1990.

Opoku, K. A. *West African Traditional Religion*, Accra et al. 1978.

Parrinder, E. G. *West African Religion*, SPCK, London 1961.

Parrinder, E. G. *African Traditional Religion*, SPCK, London 1962.

Parrinder, E. G. *African Mythology*, Hamlyn, London 1967.

Parrinder, E. G. *Religion in Africa*, Penguin, Harmondsworth 1969.

Pauw, B. A. *Religion in a Tswana Chiefdom*, Oxford University Press, London 1960.

Quarcoopome, T. N. O. *West African Traditional Religion*, Ibadan 1987.

Ranger, T. O. and Kimambo, I., eds., *The Historical Study of African Religion*, London 1972.

Rattray, R. S. *Religion and Art in Ashanti*, Clarendon Press, Oxford 1927.

Ruud, J. *Taboo: a Study of Malagasy Customs and Beliefs*, London 1960.

Sawyerr, H. *God: Ancestor or Creator?*, Longman, London 1970.

Setiloane, G. *The Image of God among the Sotho-Tswana*, Rotterdam 1976.

Smith, E. W., ed. *African Ideas of God*, Lutterworth, London 1961.

Sundermeier, T. *Nur gemeinsam können wir leben*, Gütersloh (Germany) 1988.

Taylor, J. V. *The Primal Vision*, SCM Press, London 1963.

Westerlund, D. *African Religion in African Scholarship*, Stockholm 1985.

Wilmore, G. S. *Black Religion and Black Radicalism*, New York 1983.

Wilson, M. *Rituals of Kinship among the Nyakyusa*, Clarendon Press, Oxford 1956.

Appendix C · Examples of African Proverbs and Wise Sayings

(out of a personal collection of more than 12,000 proverbs)

1. A big goat does not sneeze without reason (Kenya).
2. A child does not laugh at the ugliness of its mother (Uganda).
3. A fig tree found on the way is enough to keep you from starving (South Africa – Azania).
4. A full stomach does not last overnight (Uganda).
5. A house that is built by God will be completed (Ethiopia).
6. A lion does not eat its own cubs (Kenya).
7. A log thrown into the water does not become a crocodile.
8. A man on the ground cannot fall (South Africa – Azania).
9. A person cannot dance well on one leg only (South Africa – Azania).
10. A stick which is far away cannot kill a snake (Uganda).
11. A sweet taste does not remain forever in the mouth (Kenya).
12. A woman is a flower in a garden; her husband is the fence around it (Ghana).
13. All that we do on earth, we shall account for kneeling in heaven (Nigeria).
14. An African should not be made to suffer the loss of an arm from a gunshot in Europe (Ghana).
15. An egg never sits on a hen (East Africa).
16. An elephant does not die of one broken rib (South Africa – Azania).
17. An elephant never fails to carry its tusk (East Africa).
18. An empty tin makes a lot of noise (Kenya).
19. An eye deceives its possessor (Kenya).
20. Axes carried in the same bag cannot avoid rattling (Kenya).
21. Cattle are born with ears, their horns grow later.
22. Cattle lick each other because they know each other (South Africa – Azania).
23. Chiefs are not chiefs to women (Uganda).
24. Children confer glory on a home (Nigeria).
25. Cunning does not last for a year (South Africa – Azania).
26. Do not abandon a child when it has an itching sore (South Africa – Azania).

27. Do not desire a woman with beautiful breasts – if you have no money (South Africa – Azania).
28. Do not laugh at the snake because it walks on its belly (South Africa – Azania).
29. Don't cut a carrying strap for a child before it is born (Kenya).
30. Faeces is the food of flies (Uganda).
31. God arranges things so that a leper's sandal breaks under the camel-foot-shrub, which provides the rope to mend it (Ghana).
32. God exercises vengeance in silence (Burundi, Rwanda).
33. God goes above any shield (Rwanda).
34. God is never in a hurry; but He is always there at the proper time (Ethiopia).
35. God is sharper than a razor (Kenya).
36. God knows the things of tomorrow (Burundi).
37. God saves the afflicted according to His will (Uganda).
38. He who eats alone, dies alone (Kenya).
39. He who finds the occasion to hurt others will be hurt by them tomorrow (South Africa – Azania).
40. He who has diarrhoea knows the direction of the door without being told (Uganda).
41. He that has never travelled thinks that his mother is the only good cook in the world (Kenya).
42. Hearts cannot be lent (South Africa – Azania).
43. Heaven never dies, only men do (South Africa – Azania).
44. Houses built close together burn together (South Africa – Azania).
45. However kind a man is, he would never give his wife away as a gift to friends (Ghana).
46. Hunger does not know an elder (or a king) (Uganda).
47. If God dishes you rice in a basket, do not wish to eat soup! (Sierra Leone).
48. If God gives you a cup of wine and an evil-minded person kicks it over, He fills it up for you again (Ghana).
49. If the calf sucks too greedily, it tears away the mother's udder (Kenya).
50. If you do not spare a day to fix a door to your room, you will waste three years searching for your money (in the room) but you will never find it (Ghana).
51. If you want to speak to God, tell it to the wind (Ghana).
52. In a community of beggars, stealing and not begging, is considered a crime (Ghana).
53. It is better to be married to an old woman than to remain unmarried (Tanzania).

54. It is not difficult to hurt, but it is difficult to repair (South Africa – Azania).
55. It is the truthful that the divinities support (Nigeria).
56. It will not hurt if your lover steps on you (Tanzania).
57. Life is when you are together, alone you are an animal (West Africa).
58. Little by little fills up the bowl (Kenya).
59. Marriage roasts (hardens) (South Africa – Azania).
60. Much roaming about deprived the male rat of its fat (Ghana).
61. Never mind if your nose is ugly, as long as you can breathe through it (Zaire).
62. No one shows a child the Supreme Being (Ghana).
63. One bird in the hand is more valuable than two in the woods (Kenya).
64. One does not follow the footprints in the water (South Africa – Azania).
65. One finger cannot kill a louse (Kenya).
66. One fly causes the whole carcass of a cow to rot (Kenya).
67. One man's stomach does not work for the stomach of somebody else (South Africa – Azania).
68. One mouth cannot drink from two calabashes at the same time (Uganda).
69. People get fed up even with honey (Uganda).
70. Rather than praise yourself, you should be praised by God (Rwanda).
71. Sleep killed the lion (South Africa – Azania).
72. Stolen things bring in misfortune (Kenya).
73. The calabash of the kind person breaks not (Nigeria).
74. The clan of *I will do it*, was overtaken without having done it (Kenya).
75. The cock in drinking water, raises its head to God in thankfulness (Ghana).
76. The creature is not greater than its Creator (Burundi).
77. The day one has plenty to eat, it is the elders who come to the rescue. The day one has nought to eat, it is the elders who come to the rescue (Nigeria).
78. The earth is the mother of all (Uganda).
79. The enemy prepares a grave, but God prepares you a way of escape (Rwanda).
80. The forest has ears (Kenya).
81. The guest has tastier snuff (Kenya).

82. The hand of the young does not reach the high shelf; that of the elder does not go into the gourd (Nigeria).
83. The hen comes from the egg and the egg comes from the hen (South Africa – Azania).
84. The hyena does not forget where it has hidden its kill (South Africa – Azania).
85. The leopard that visits you is the one which kills you (East Africa).
86. The mother of a great man has no horns (i.e. she is a simple woman) (Kenya).
87. The mouth is the radio (transmitter) of the African (Kenya).
88. The one who is too talkative leaves his mouth empty (East Africa).
89. The one whom God clothes will not go naked (Ethiopia).
90. The plant protected by God is never hurt by the wind (Rwanda).
91. The poor man's main tool is his tongue with which he defends himself (Ghana).
92. The stick of God does not cause one to cry (i.e. it is not painful) (Kenya).
93. The strength of the crocodile is the water (South Africa – Azania).
94. The warmth of a rock is known only by the lizard (which lies on it) (Kenya).
95. The way to overcome cold is to warm each other (South Africa – Azania).
96. The wealth of the wicked will be scattered by the wind like chaff (South Africa – Azania).
97. The woman is a banana tree (which multiplies itself); the man, however, is a cornstalk (which stands alone) (Ghana).
98. The woman is the rib of man (Uganda).
99. There is no difference between mother and baby snakes, they are equally poisonous (Kenya).
100. There is no lion which cannot miss a chase (Kenya).
101. There is no pond which the sun cannot dry up (Kenya).
102. 'Though I am not edible', says the vulture, 'yet I nurse my eggs in the branches of a high tree because man is hard to be trusted' (Ghana).
103. To avoid fraud (or since God does not like wickedness), God gave every creature a name (Ghana).
104. To borrow is to spoil friendship (East Africa).
105. To eat much leaves you with a swollen belly (Kenya).
106. To stir (the water in) the pond brings up the mud (South Africa – Azania).
107. Two friends share the white ant (Uganda).

108. Two male hippos do not stay in the same pond (South Africa – Azania).
109. We are born from the womb of our mother; we are buried in the womb of the earth (Ethiopia).
110. We do not see God, we only see His works (Ethiopia).
111. Wealth is dew (South Africa – Azania).
112. What God puts in store for someone (or preserves for the poor) never goes rotten (East Africa).
113. When a sweet potato has been thrown into the ash-heap it becomes uneatable (South Africa – Azania).
114. When the chief limps, all his subjects limp also (South Africa – Azania).
115. Whenever a person breaks a stick in the forest, let him consider what it would feel like, if it were himself that was thus broken (Nigeria).
116. Whoever comes last drinks muddy water (Kenya, Uganda).
117. Wives and oxen have no friends (Kenya).
118. Yam is sweet, but one should eat it in the normal way, lest over-swallowing chokes him (Ghana).
119. You can trust neither the rainy season sky nor babies' bottoms (Ethiopia).

Sources for the proverbs:
Bannerman, J. Y., *Mfantse-Akan Mbebusem (Ghanaian Proverbs)*, Accra 1974.
Barra, G., *1000 Kikuyu Proverbs*, London & Nairobi 1960.
Bartels, L. *Oromo Religion*, Berlin 1983.
Dalfovo, A. T., *Lögbara Proverbs*, Rome 1984.
Idowu, E. B., *Olodumare – God in Yoruba Belief*, London 1962.
Junod, H. P., *Vutlhari Bya Vatsonga (Tsonga Proverbs)*, 2nd edn., Pretoria 1957.
Kalugila, L., *Swahili Proverbs from East Africa*, Uppsala 1977.
Kimilu, D. N., *Mukamba Wa Wo*, Nairobi 1962.
Mbiti, J. S., private collection and various publications.
Opoku, K. A., *West African Traditional Religion*, Accra et al. 1978.
p'Bitek, O., *Acholi Proverbs*, Nairobi 1985.

· Index

separated from men
85–6; unknowable and
unchanging 59; *see also*
spirits
good: behaviour 177–8,
179; God 55; medicine
men 156–7; *see also*
morals
graves *see* burial
groves 64–5, 150, 152

harvest rituals 135–6
health 139–40, 155; *see
also* disease; medicine
heaven/sky 35–7; and
death 123; and earth
36–7, 61, 85–6; and
God 45, 46–7; men
from 83; spirits 70, 71–2
hereafter 70, 75–9,
128–30; *see also* spirits
heritage 2–10, 13–14
hills 152
Hinduism 33, 187
history 2–10, 13–14
holiness of God 55–6
homestead rituals 140
hospitality, duty of 176
humans 14–16; at centre
of universe 36, 43–4;
created 35, 82–6;
images of God 53–4;
names 28; ruler as
symbol 163–4;
sacrificed 138; spirits
70, 75–9; *see also* life
husbands *see* marriage

ideas 199
illness *see* disease
images of God 53–4
immortality 85, 105, 111,
116
inheritance 115
initiation 96–103, 104
intermediaries 68–9
Islam 14, 17, 184–6,
188–9, 197; and death
121, 126; distribution
30–1, 32–3

Jainism 187
Judaism 33, 186–7

kings, queens and chiefs

5–6, 12, 16–17, 68;
authority 42; funerals
81, 121; and God 162;
God as 52; and rituals
140–1
kinship 107; *see also*
marriage

lakes *see* water
leaders 12–13, 77,
153–64; ritual *see*
diviners, elders,
medicine men, priests,
rain-makers; traditional
see kings
legends *see* myths
libations 45, 148; *see also*
sacrifices
life and life events
15–16, 29–30, 200–1;
and naming 93, 94–5;
rhythms of 36, 37; *see
also* birth; death;
initiation; marriage;
rituals
limitations: God's lack of
58; of people 45–6, 201
living dead 70, 77–9,
125–6; as
intermediaries 66, 68–9;
remembering 128–30

magic, sorcery and
witchcraft 19, 42–3,
117, 165–71
man *see* humans
marriage and family life
104–15, 145; customs
106–110; dead
members *see* living
dead; gifts 108; and
initiation 99; meaning
of 110–12; morals
175–6; multiple 8, 112;
obligation to marry
104–6; *see also* children
medicine 170–3; and
death 127, 130; *see also*
disease; health
medicine men and
women 12, 21, 68, 91,
153–7; and spirits 79,
80, 126
mediums *see* diviners
migration 3, 14, 27

misfortune *see* calamities
morals and values 12, 41,
174–9, 198; community
176–8; family 175–6;
and God 178–9; moral
order 40–1; *see also* evil;
good
mother 53; *see also* babies
mountains 152
multiple births 95–6
multiple marriages 8, 112
music and dance 3–4, 9,
25–7, 66–8, 82, 121–2
Muslims *see* Islam
mystical order 41–3
myths and legends 8, 8,
50, 61; creation 82–6;
death 116–18; and
spirits 71, 76–7

naming: child 28, 92–5,
130; God 47–9, 94
nature: and belief in God
46–7; laws of 40; spirits
70, 71–5; *see also*
universe
numbers, ritual 146

objects 11–12, 24, 43,
144–7, 167, 169
offerings *see* sacrifices
oracles 68, 80, 159
oral tradition 4–5, 8, 79,
82
order in universe 40–3
other religions 180–93; *see
also in particular*
Christianity; Islam

paganism 19
paradise, loss of 86
parents 53; *see also*
children
people *see* humans
places 11–12, 20–4,
147–52; names 28; and
sacrifice 64–5
polygamy 8, 112
possession, spirit 126–7
power: of God 56; in
universe 40–3
prayers 20, 53, 61–3, 91,
134; and sacrifice 64,
66, 68
pregnancy 87–9, 132, 145

214

• Acknowledgements

The author and publisher would like to thank the following for permission to reproduce photographs in this book:

The Ancient Art and Architecture Collection for pp 7, 13, 164 © Ronald Sheridan; Lambert Bartels for p 89; A. & C. Black for p 154 from *The Essential Kaffir* by D. Kidd (1904); Hilary Bradt for p 125; Revd. Dr. A. B. T. Byaruhanga-Akiiki for p 98; Charlotte Covill for p 5; Carrie Craig for p 150; Gyldendal for pp 101, 195; Mrs Simikha Harjula for p 129; Jane Harley for p 6; Revd. J. O. Kayode for pp 67, 99; Kyeni Mbiti for pp 74 (1989), 151; Nationfoto: East African Newspapers Ltd., for p 156; Joseph Ndirangu for p 158; Rex Features Ltd for p 51 (bottom); Routledge and Sons for p 123 from *Pagan Tribes of the Nilotic Sudan* by G. G. and B. Z. Seligman (1932); S.O.A.S. for pp 22, 23, 24 from *Das Buch der Schrift* by Carl Faulman (Kaiserlich-Königliche, 1880), pp 38, 39 from *The Language of Adinkra Patterns* by A. K. Quarcoo (Institute of African Studies, University of Ghana, 1972); Dr Doris Wagner for pp 97, 106.

Grateful acknowledgement is also made to the owners of articles who kindly allowed the author to photograph the items which appear on the following pages;

Rt. Revd. Bishop Y. K. Bamunoba for pp 80, 127, 145; Revd. Professor P. Frank de Graeve for pp 42, 100 (top), 169; The Institute of American Studies (University of Ibadan) for p 183; Mrs Susanne Weiger (Adunni Olorisa) and her associates for their works which appear in photographs on pp 58, 68.

We would also like to thank the following for permission to reproduce line illustrations in this book:

Mrs Susan Denyer for p 26; John Gilkes for p 31.

The author and publishers have made every effort to trace copyright holders. In the event of anyone having been inadvertently overlooked or incorrectly cited, we shall be very glad to hear from you and make the necessary changes at the first opportunity.